Red Valkyries

Red Valkyries

Feminist Lessons from Five Revolutionary Women

Kristen R. Ghodsee

VERSO

London • New York

First published by Verso 2022
© Kristen R. Ghodsee 2022

1 3 5 7 9 10 8 6 4 2

Verso
UK: 6 Meard Street, London W1F 0EG
US: 20 Jay Street, Suite 1010, Brooklyn, NY 11201
versobooks.com

Verso is the imprint of New Left Books

ISBN-13: 978-1-83976-660-2

ISBN-13: 978-1-83976-663-3 (US EBK)

ISBN-13: 978-1-83976-662-6 (UK EBK)

British Library Cataloguing in Publication Data
A catalogue record for this book is available from the British Library

Library of Congress Cataloging-in-Publication Data
A catalog record for this book is available from the Library of Congress
Printed and bound by CPI Group (UK) Ltd, Croydon, CR0 4YY

Typeset in Sabon by MJ & N Gavan, Truro, Cornwall
Printed and bound by CPI Group (UK) Ltd, Croydon CR0 4YY

For Daisy,
because canines can be comrades, too

Contents

List of Figures

Author's Note

Both Russian and Bulgarian are Slavic languages written in the Cyrillic alphabet, and many competing conventions exist regarding the romanization of Cyrillic letters into the Latin alphabet. The Cyrillic letter "Й" can be transliterated as the Latin letters "j," "i," or "y," which means that Alexandra Kollontai's last name can be spelled Kollontaj, Kollontai, or Kollontay. The Cyrillic letter "Я" can be transliterated as a combination of the Latin letters "ja," "ia," "ya," or the unwieldy "iā," meaning that Krupskaya can be Krupskaja, Krupskaia, or Krupskaiā. Similarly, the Cyrillic letter "Ю" can be Romanized as "ju," "yu," or "iu," giving us Ljudmila, Lyudmila, or Liudmila. Generally speaking, I try to be consistent with the romanization of names, but unfortunately, my English language sources use different romanization conventions and so there will be inconsistencies in the text when I use direct quotes. I also try to use the popular romanized spellings of more familiar names like Trotsky or Tolstoy, and I generally use the anglicized versions of Russian names that are more familiar to readers (such as Leo Tolstoy rather than Lev Tolstoy). Finally, in some Slavic languages, surnames have masculine and feminine endings: Lyudmila Pavlichenko's maiden name was Belova, but her father's was Belov. In the same way, Krupskaya was the daughter of a Krupsky and Lagadinova was the daughter of a Lagadinov.

Dates in tsarist Russia are often confusing to Western readers because of the differences between the Julian and the Gregorian calendars. In Europe, the Julian calendar came into effect in 45 BCE and was the primary calendar of the Roman

Empire and throughout medieval Europe for about 1,600 years. Unfortunately, the mathematical and astronomical calculations on which the calendar was based were a bit off, and it picked up an extra day every 128 years. In 1582, Pope Gregory XIII issued a papal bull that created a new Gregorian calendar, which is the calendar that Western countries use today. The Russian Orthodox Church never accepted this Roman Catholic calendrical reform, however, and continued to use the old Julian calendar. Significant events in Russian history, therefore, have been named according to their dates on the Julian calendar, which can be confusing to Western readers; the 1917 "October revolution," for example, took place on November 7 by the Gregorian calendar (October 25 by the Julian calendar), and the "February revolution" that same year lasted from March 8 to March 12 (February 24 to 28). I use terms such as "October revolution" in this text but all dates listed are according to the Gregorian calendar.

Note that the Russian city of Saint Petersburg was renamed Petrograd in 1914. After Lenin's death in 1924, the city became Leningrad. In 1991, it reverted to Saint Petersburg. I use all three names in the text, depending on the time of the events I am describing.

I use the terms "state socialism" and "state socialist" to refer to the governments of the Soviet Union and Bulgaria during the twentieth century. Although ruled by "communist" parties, both nations considered themselves to be in the socialist stage of the Marxist developmental framework, in which "communism" was the ideal society toward which they were striving. They referred to themselves as "socialist" states, or societies living under what they called "really-existing socialism," to distinguish their still imperfect systems from the communist ideal. This is why the USSR stands for the Union of Soviet *Socialist* Republics and why the ruling party in East Germany was called the *Socialist* Unity Party. In no East European country was the goal of communism achieved, nor did any state claim to have achieved it, and so I prefer to avoid this term. However, Western scholars and politicians tend to use the terms "communist" and "communism" to refer to these countries. To the extent that these words appear in this book, they can be more or less used interchangeably with "socialist" and "socialism," although there exist important theoretical and practical differences between the two political frameworks. Also, it is common among women's historians to refer to women like Kollontai as "socialist feminists," "Marxist feminists," and "left feminists," even though Kollontai herself rejected the term "feminist" throughout her life. Where possible, I have used the term "socialist women's activists" instead. The use of the word "feminist" in the subtitle of this book was the decision of the Verso marketing department.

My use of terms such as "woman" and "man," "male" and "female," and "mother" and "father" in these pages primarily denote categories as they were understood within the context of the struggles of nineteenth- and twentieth-century socialist women's activists in Eastern Europe, even as I recognize that these words are used more inclusively today. These activists focused their revolutionary efforts on the emancipation of what are now called cisgender women, most of whom were assumed to be heterosexual and interested in becoming mothers. The experiences and political interests of queer, trans, and nonbinary people at the time don't make an appearance, not because they are unimportant, but rather because they merit more attention than I can devote to them here.

I have tried to be sensitive to ableist and other outdated language in my own prose, but where it appears in direct quotations, I have left it unaltered.

I have included citations in the endnotes for direct quotations and statistical figures. Most readers can feel free to ignore these citations unless they are interested in a particular source or the clarification of a specific term or historical event. The Timeline of Key Events gives readers a sense of how the lives of these five women intersected with major global events such as World War I, the Russian revolution, World War II, and the Cold War.

Finally, because this entire book was written during the COVID-19 lockdowns in 2020 and 2021, I relied heavily on digitally-accessible or internet-orderable primary and secondary sources for the four Russian/Soviet women. These introductory biographical essays only provide an initial glimpse into the fascinating lives of these five Red Valkyries. The many sources cited in the endnotes and in the Suggestions for Further Reading are a good place to start for readers who wish to dive deeper.

Timeline of Key Events

1861 – Emancipation of the Russian serfs

1863 – Publication of Nikolai Chernyshevsky's novel *What Is to Be Done?*

1869 – Nadezhda Krupskaya born

1870 – Vladimir Ilyich Ulyanov (Lenin) born

1872 – Alexandra Kollontai born

1874 – Inessa Armand born

1878 – Bulgarian independence from the Ottoman Empire

1881 – Assassination of Tsar Alexander II of Russia

1894 – Publication of Leo Tolstoy's *The Kingdom of God Is Within You*

1905 – Bloody Sunday in Russia

1914 – Beginning of World War I

1916 – Lyudmila Pavlichenko born

1917 – February revolution in Russia/abdication of the tsar
Lenin, Krupskaya, Armand, and Kollontai all return from exile to Russia
October revolution in Russia/Lenin and the Bolsheviks seize power

1918 – Treaty of Brest-Litovsk takes Russia out of World War I with large territorial losses
World War I ends with the loss of the Central Powers

1919 – Rosa Luxemburg and Karl Liebknecht murdered in Germany

1920 – Inessa Armand dies

1923 – Russian civil war ends

1924 – Vladimir Lenin dies

1930 – Elena Lagadinova born

1933 – Hitler becomes Chancellor of Germany

1939 – World War II begins

Nadezhda Krupskaya dies

Molotov-Ribbentrop treaty signed (non-aggression pact between the USSR and Germany)

1941 – Bulgaria signs the Tripartite Pact and joins the Axis powers

Germany invades the Soviet Union, which then declares war on the Axis powers

Lyudmila Pavlichenko joins the Red Army as a sniper

Elena Lagadinova begins helping the Bulgarian partisans

1942 – Lyudmila Pavlichenko tours the United States, Canada, and Great Britain and befriends Eleanor Roosevelt

1944 – Elena Lagadinova becomes the youngest female partisan in Bulgaria

September 9 coup d'état/uprising in Bulgaria

Bulgaria switches sides in World War II

Normandy landings (D-Day)

1945 – World War II ends

1952 – Alexandra Kollontai dies

1956 – Nikita Khrushchev delivers his Secret Speech denouncing the crimes of Stalin

1968 – Elena Lagadinova becomes the president of the Committee of the Bulgarian Women's Movement

1974 – Lyudmila Pavlichenko dies

1975 – Elena Lagadinova leads the Bulgarian delegation to the United Nations First World Conference on Women for International Women's Year in Mexico City

1985 – Elena Lagadinova leads the Bulgarian delegation to the United Nations Third World Conference on Women in Nairobi, Kenya

1989 – Fall of the Berlin Wall

State socialism ends in Bulgaria

1990 – Elena Lagadinova forced into retirement

1991 – Breakup of the Soviet Union and end of the Cold War
2017 – Centennial of the Russian revolution
Elena Lagadinova dies

Introduction

Bourgeois Feminism and Its Discontents

"Sex and Socialism." That's the name of the university class I started teaching back in 2003. Over fourteen or fifteen weeks, an interdisciplinary assortment of students and I embark on a semester-long discussion of the relationship between capitalism, socialism, and women's emancipation. When I first offered this course at a small liberal arts college in Maine almost twenty years ago, socialism as a political ideology had been largely consigned to the dustbin of history. After the fall of the Berlin Wall in 1989, Western triumphalism, Clintonomics, and the dot-com boom of the roaring nineties purportedly gave proof to the fantasy that liberal democracy and capitalism represented the "end of history."[1] Even social democratic countries in Western Europe shrunk their social safety nets and pared back public spending and laws protecting workers' rights. In the UK, Prime Minister Tony Blair removed Clause IV (calling for the common ownership of industry) from Labour's constitution in 1994, abandoning the party's semi-Marxist roots. My curious course on "sex and socialism" provided little more than a glance backward at a utopian project considered obsolete.

When I moved to the University of Pennsylvania in 2017, the political context had shifted. The global financial crisis, the Occupy Wall Street protests, and the near success of Bernie Sanders in the 2016 Democratic Party primary piqued renewed curiosity about alternatives to capitalism. My first course offered at Penn was "Sex and Socialism," cross-listed with

Gender, Sexuality, and Women's Studies (GSWS). As before, my students and I investigated difficult questions by reading primary texts from the eighteenth-, nineteenth-, and twentieth-century thinkers who took a critical view of the supposedly free markets for human labor that followed the abolition of slavery and serfdom. Do rates of remuneration fairly compensate individual productivity? How do racist and sexist stereotypes about certain groups in society and imperfect information perpetuate inequalities in labor markets? And how have different proponents of various types of socialism historically sought to mitigate or abolish these inequities? To answer these questions, I often teach about the lives of women and men who have counted themselves among the enemies of capitalism.

In this book, you'll meet five of them. Lyudmila Pavlichenko: the world's most successful woman sniper with 309 confirmed kills in World War II. Alexandra Kollontai: the first Soviet Commissar of Social Welfare and a champion of sex positivity before we even had a phrase for it. Nadezhda Krupskaya: realizing the revolution through a radical expansion of education, literacy, and librarianship. Inessa Armand: the head of what was essentially the first ministry of women's affairs in the Soviet Union. And, finally, Elena Lagadinova: the youngest female partisan fighting against her Axis-allied government in World War II and the president of the Committee of the Bulgarian Women's Movement for twenty-two years. Although they each played a crucial role in forging new opportunities for hundreds of millions of women across the globe, their contributions get lost because they supported a type of women's activism that most Westerners have never heard of. I will never forget a conversation I had in the fall of 2017 with a fourth-year student who lingered after class. As we chatted about the day's lecture, she shook her head and said, "I'm graduating this spring and I can't believe I could have earned a GSWS major without ever having heard of Nadezhda Krupskaya or Alexandra Kollontai."

I sighed. To this day, Western feminists dominate the historiography of the global women's movement. Early champions of women's rights such as the English Mary Wollstonecraft and John Stuart Mill and the French Olympe de Gouges focused on individual rights. They asserted that, since women and men shared an inherent capacity to reason, differences between the sexes arose from differential socialization rather than from women's supposed "natural" inferiority. Access to education and the ability to make a living outside of marriage could liberate women from both ignorance and servitude. Activists in the late nineteenth and early twentieth centuries such as Susan B. Anthony and Elizabeth Cady Stanton in the United States and Emmeline Pankhurst in the United Kingdom built on these ideas to demand women's right to vote. Images of the suffragists animate the popular imagination as representatives of what is sometimes referred to as the "first wave" of feminism. In 1979, for example, the United States Mint chose Susan B. Anthony for its first coin featuring the image of an American woman. In 1999, *Time* magazine named Emmeline Pankhurst one of the "100 most important people of the twentieth century" for her role in winning women the franchise.

Western feminist icons of the so-called "second wave" included Simone de Beauvoir (author of *The Second Sex*), Betty Friedan (author of *The Feminine Mystique*), and Gloria Steinem (the founder of *Ms.* magazine). Like their "first wave" predecessors, these women largely focused on attaining increased rights and privileges for individual women. In her 1963 book, widely viewed as responsible for launching the U.S. women's movement, Betty Friedan focused on the idea of "self-actualization," a concept borrowed from the work of the American psychologist Abraham Maslow and his theory of the hierarchy of needs.[2] Maslow argued that physiological needs like food and shelter form the base of a pyramid of human necessities. Once these needs are met, people can climb up the pyramid by seeking out safety, love and belonging, and esteem. Self-actualization (the individualistic fulfillment of one's inherent potential) is the apex of Maslow's pyramid. Although scholars critiqued Maslow's ethnocentric hierarchy for valorizing a hyper-individualism alien to many communally oriented societies,[3] Friedan and other "second wave" feminists believed that the pursuit of "self-actualization" should be the primary goal of a feminist movement.[4] More recently, women such as Facebook COO Sheryl Sandberg have advocated for women's corporate advancement, admonishing individual women and girls to "lean in" and break through the remaining barriers that hinder their full equality with men.

But from the earliest days of the development of what we call feminism, there existed an entirely different group of women who, while agreeing that women have the same innate capacity for reason as men and are therefore deserving of political rights, fought side by side with their male counterparts to create a more equitable world for all through collective action. Women in Russia, for example, achieved the franchise in 1917 before most women in the West, and full coeducational access to all universities in Eastern Europe predated that in the United States by decades. Furthermore, women joined the labor force and entered traditionally male professions beginning in the 1920s, and by the 1930s and 1940s, Soviet women were earning doctoral degrees in physics and other natural sciences. A 1957 report of the American Manpower Planning Council noted, with some dismay, that "there are annually some 13,000 women graduating as engineers in the Soviet Union, compared to well under 100 in the United States."[5] Although they did not have what we in the West would think of as a feminist movement, socialist women enjoyed rapid gains in societies where states made explicit commitments to promoting women's economic independence through the radical expansion of social safety nets and special programs to support working mothers.[6]

4

Despite these achievements, most Western historians and gender scholars have ignored or downplayed the profound importance of socialists in shaping twentieth-century women's movements. Even the most prominent of these—Alexandra Kollontai, a theorist, teacher, speaker, politician, and diplomat who served as one of the first female ambassadors in the world and was twice nominated for the Nobel Peace Prize—barely gets mentioned in Western textbooks. Her work is completely absent from the 2005 *Feminist Theory: A Philosophical Anthology*, the 2016 edition of the *Oxford Handbook of Feminist Theory*, and the 2016 (fourth) and 2021 (fifth) editions of the Routledge *Feminist Theory Reader*. Kollontai's unrelenting antagonism to capitalism apparently undermines her credentials as a "feminist theorist" in liberal circles, even though her ideas and her power to implement them as a politician in the early years of the Soviet Union arguably did more to realize women's full emancipation than the works or deeds of any other woman in the twentieth century (including Emmeline Pankhurst!).

Kollontai and the other women considered in this book placed themselves on the socialist side of the liberal versus socialist feminism divide (also referred to as "difference" versus "equality" feminism or "relational" versus "individualist" feminism).[7] Many of these early thinkers were highly idealistic and questioned common ideas about the naturalness and inevitability of how labor markets were structured while, at the same time, trying to protect workers from the contemporary ravages of industrial capitalism. Although they often agreed with the initial aims of the liberal feminists, they felt these goals did not go far enough to help the majority of women in their societies. In nineteenth-century Britain, for instance, the right to vote was based on ownership of a certain amount of property and excluded all women. While suffragists focused on removing the sex exclusion, a different group of women agitated for the removal of the property qualifications, arguing that voting access for only propertied women was a purely middle-class demand.[8]

Conflict between liberal and socialist goals in the fight for gender equality has continued into the twenty-first century. Consider, for example, Hasbro's 2019 creation of the mascot Ms. Monopoly—"Mr. Monopoly's niece and a self-made investment guru"—as a celebration of women's empowerment. With her black, high-heeled pumps, sleek gray blazer, and a disposable coffee cup labeled "boss," Ms. Monopoly represents the logical conclusion of Facebook COO Sheryl Sandberg's brand of "lean in" politics whereby women win the game by becoming ruthless monopolists just like their male competitors.

In the Ms. Monopoly version of the Monopoly board game, all of the properties are inventions or products developed or designed by women. Instead of controlling Broadway and Park Place, players can buy Chocolate Chip Cookies and Stem Cell Isolation. Most importantly, players who identify as female collect $240 after passing go, whereas players who identify as male only get $200, leading Hasbro to brag that Ms. Monopoly is "the first game where women make more than men."[9] This #girlboss feminism ignores the fact that, due to a lack of opportunities, connections, and resources, the vast majority of women have few chances of becoming self-made investment gurus and joining the economic elite. And are we really supposed to believe that Ms. Monopoly is "self-made" when Mr. Monopoly is her uncle?

"Lean in" feminism and #girlboss online activism fail to address the structural inequalities that continue to perpetuate sexism no matter how many women find their way into the C-Suite. Liberal feminism, in fact, often increases these inequalities by creating private clubs like The Wing which commodify exclusive access to women's networks in the name of empowerment.[10] Similarly, women-centered investment funds like Ellevest, a financial services company "built by women, for women," encourages risk-averse women to participate in the stock market in order to close the "investment gap" with men. Ellevest Private Wealth also offers a feminist version of "private wealth management for high and ultra high net worth individuals, families, and institutions."[11] While it is true that "old boys' clubs" perpetuate discrimination against women, liberal feminist projects like The Wing and Ellevest can only benefit a handful of women at most. With about 21 million American women living in poverty in 2018, Ellevest's brand of women's empowerment clearly ignores the needs of a large population of workers without savings to invest.[12]

While the challenges faced by working women are widespread, the burdens caused by gender inequity fall disproportionately on the poor, especially immigrant communities and communities of color. My own grandmother came to the United States from Puerto Rico in 1947 and gave birth to my mother two years later. Abandoned by her husband, my grandmother worked as a seamstress to support herself in the New York City garment industry. Lacking any form of social support or reliable childcare, my grandmother arranged for my mother to live with her grandparents back in Sabana Grande. When circumstances compelled my five-year-old mother back to New York, my Catholic grandmother sent her to live with the Baptistine nuns in their orphanage at St. Lucy's School in Newark, New Jersey.

My grandmother left my mother with the Baptistines for *eight years* until my mother turned thirteen. "Grandma would come and visit maybe once or twice a month when she had money to come and see me," my seventy-two-year-old mother recently recalled to me in a text message. "But at times she did not come for months if she did not feel well or didn't have a ride to come see me." Until her death in September 2021, my ninety-three-year-old grandmother and my mother still fought over my mother's childhood. My mother resented the abandonment and melted down in tears when asked about her life at St. Lucy's, while my grandmother swore that she had no choice but to put her there, and that she did her best to give my mother a better quality of life and education than she would have had living with my grandmother in Washington Heights. Where my mother blamed my grandmother for her individual choices, my grandmother blamed the system that made it impossible for her to work and care for my mother at the same time.

The tension between women's interests on the basis of their gender versus their economic interests defined competing brands of activism throughout the twentieth century. Alexandra Kollontai and other socialists perceived those who called themselves feminists as representing the fortunate Ms. Monopolys of the world, or what the German women's activist Clara Zetkin referred to as "the upper ten thousand."[13] As in Britain, liberal feminists often fought to increase their own rights and privileges, arguing that incremental gains for wealthy women in the short term would eventually trickle down to all women. For socialist women, however, this liberal feminist strategy represented a threat to the long-term success of progressive movements because it harbored the potential to divide the working class and forestall what they saw as an inevitable progression beyond capitalism. Where many feminist movements tended to organize women separately to win access to the rights and privileges of a political and economic system reserved for men, socialist activists challenged the underlying system that created and legitimated the unequal distribution of privilege to begin with.

Socialist women's activists understood that capitalists benefitted from women's oppression and would therefore fiercely resist demands that might erode their profit margins. When women fed, clothed, nursed, and nurtured the workers and future workers in their families, they provided an invaluable service to those who employed those workers, who could thus off-load the costs of maintaining healthy employees onto the private sphere. Attempts to value this labor through higher taxes on corporations or by promoting worker ownership and control of productive enterprises posed a threat to business owners. But these same business owners could extend some morsels of formal equality to wealthy women without changing the more fundamental structures that oppressed working women (such as property requirements for voting access). Socialist women complained that the liberal feminist approach—creating independent women's organizations to promote formal equality—obsessed over access to a few spindly trees while missing the entire forest. And, in the particular context of tsarist Russia in the late nineteenth and early twentieth centuries, Kollontai and her contemporaries believed that men and women had to work together to generate the numerical strength necessary to overthrow the tsar. This debate between socialist women's activists and liberal feminists continues to this day.

Where liberal feminists often focused on legal equality, women's activists on the farther left advocated for equity through the expansion of social safety nets in the short term and for a more just economic system in the long term. In addition to the franchise, access to education, and labor force opportunities, socialists demanded the expansion of paid maternity leave with job protection and free or subsidized childcare to support working parents. Liberal feminists disliked these objectives for reinforcing the expectation that women bear and raise children, and some encouraged fathers to "lean in" to care work within the family.[14] Socialist women's activists sympathized with these aims but recognized that the traditional idea of mothers as primary caregivers would not be overturned so easily. They chose to focus, therefore, not on achieving a more equitable distribution of unpaid care work *within* the nuclear family or encouraging wealthy women to hire other (often poorer) women to perform domestic labor in the private sphere, but on the distribution of care work across a wider network of potential caregivers supported by the allocation of public funds.

While special programs for mothers might reinforce social expectations that certain members of society are more "naturally" suited to care work, fancy new laws guaranteeing *de facto* equality do not miraculously erase those expectations. Although some countries legally mandate parental leave (available to parents of all genders), new mothers consistently take longer leaves than new fathers.[15] Nor can legal codes sway the market mechanisms that exacerbate inequalities between workers with and without care obligations. Employers use statistical averages about groups of workers who are more or less likely to leave the labor market, sorting potential employees into "reliable" and "less reliable" categories[16] and paying those in the "less reliable" category lower wages. In monogamous families with only two parents, when one parent is forced to stay home to look after young children or elderly relatives (due to a lack of child or elder care), couples rationally choose the parent with the lower wage. But, if one particular category of worker is always the one to leave the labor market and stay home (mothers) then that very choice reinforces the stereotype that they are "less reliable" workers and therefore deserving of a lower wage. This cycle repeats itself ad infinitum. Unless we change the system.

Although debates between liberal and socialist feminism have historically revolved around issues of pregnancy, childbirth, and childcare, and some socialist feminists have embraced a natalist stance that many would find distasteful today (that is, believing that all women *should* be mothers), one can accept the value of their proposals around public provision of services without condoning their more traditional ideals about parenthood. In a capitalist economy, one obvious way of avoiding market discrimination against parents is to remain childless, and some might have compelling political and environmental reasons for choosing this option. Others might prefer to organize their private lives into more capacious, non-consanguine, multigenerational networks of care and comradeship without societal support. But we must not ignore the current reality that many adults still want to become parents and raise families in more conventional ways. Rather than deriding their supposed false consciousness or stubborn attachment to the nuclear family, we should be sympathetic about the difficulty of doing so in an increasingly precarious gig economy with few social safety nets (and, at least in the United States, crushing levels of student and consumer debt).

Efforts to address this difficulty, however, are complicated by the conflicting political demands of different classes of potential parents. More privileged parents might reject special treatment as parents because they fear it will limit their ability to advance within their chosen professions. In contrast to specific parental protections, legal equality for all workers increases opportunities for economic advancement, which allows privileged parents more resources with which to hire less advantaged workers (almost always women and usually women of color) to do the domestic work the professional parents no longer have the time or inclination to do themselves. In an economic system which favors those who start the game with the tallest pile of cash, a narrow concern with legal equality between the sexes primarily benefits the wives and daughters of the existing elites who have access to the financial resources to benefit most from these opportunities. Ms. Monopoly wants the opportunity to make more money so she can hire a better nanny. In contrast, laws or policies which support *the public provision* of services specifically for working parents allow for the redistribution of societal resources to support a higher standard of living for the whole population and not just those lucky enough to rise to the top. How much happier, I often wonder, would my mother's childhood have been if my grandmother could have dropped her off at a daycare center attached to the garment factory or if a local elementary school had provided a free afterschool program?

In the end, demands for procedural equality rather than specific parental services coexist easily with capitalism because they require few resources. Promoting women into executive positions may save their employers money (as women are generally paid less than men) and appointing more women onto corporate boards may actually increase profits for corporations.[17] The expansion of social services, on the other hand, costs money, and that means raising taxes or promoting more radical means of redistribution and thereby reducing private profits. A more fundamental way to fight the discrimination against parents embedded in competitive labor markets is to challenge the system that makes it so difficult for people to become parents and raise children. This is why the Red Valkyries attacked the capitalist economic structure that created these imbalances in the first place, and why their stories have been largely ignored by history books and in university classrooms. Learning about the lives and works of these revolutionary women of Eastern Europe illustrates both how and why liberal feminism became "capitalism's handmaiden."[18]

The unique geopolitics of the Cold War exacerbated the longstanding tension between liberal and socialist feminists. The conflict extended to include the "woman question," as it was called in many socialist countries, and this became an important node of superpower rivalry[19]: whether capitalism or socialism could be more successful at increasing opportunities for women's emancipation. To better understand the global context of these ongoing debates, I have spent the last twenty-five years immersed in ethnographic and historical research about women's emancipation in Eastern Europe before, during, and after the Cold War. I have written eight books and many articles and essays about the gendered aspects of ordinary life in Eastern Europe and what the socialist path to women's emancipation looked like in practice. Since January 2019, I have hosted a podcast on the life and work of Alexandra Kollontai and spoken in popular media about socialist feminism, women's issues, and East European history.

This book builds on my previous work and focuses specifically on four women from Russia/Soviet Union and one woman from Bulgaria (the Balkan country where I have conducted most of my primary research over the years). Despite my focus on Eastern Europe, I want to acknowledge the diverse and wide-ranging history of socialist and communist women's activism, which includes individuals from many countries outside of this region. If I had more time (and more pages), I could include important figures like Flora Tristan (France/Peru), Dolores Ibárruri (Spain), Claudia Jones (Trinidad and Tobago), Thyra Edwards (USA), Maryam Firouz (Iran), Jessie Street (Australia), Nguyễn Thị Bình (Vietnam), Vilma Espín (Cuba), Rosario Morales (Puerto Rico), Deng Yingchao (China), Aoua Keita (Mali), Funmilayo Ransome-Kuti (Nigeria), Hertta Kuusinen (Finland), Umi Sardjono (Indonesia), Kanak Mukherjee (India), Naziha al-Dulaimi (Iraq), and Iijima Aiko (Japan), among many others. I hope the mini biographies in these pages inspire further research and writing on the many other lives worthy of study, particularly those of women of color in the West and those struggling for justice in the Global South.

We must all write what we know best; as a professor of Russian and East European Studies, I focused my efforts on five of the women I've taught about for almost two decades. I chose Lyudmila Pavlichenko because, over the years, my students always seemed the most fascinated by the remarkable achievements of her life, and because she forged a close friendship with American first lady Eleanor Roosevelt and

*A monument celebrating men and women partisans
during World War II in Sofia, Bulgaria*

became something of a celebrity when she visited the United States in 1942. I included Alexandra Kollontai because of my fascination with her life and work, and Nadezhda Krupskaya and Inessa Armand because they were Kollontai's comrades in exile before the Bolshevik revolution and her primary accomplices in crafting Soviet policy on women's issues in the years immediately following 1917. Finally, I count Elena Lagadinova among these Red Valkyries because I had the honor and privilege of interviewing her over the course of seven years between 2010 and 2017. In the pages that follow, I provide a short outline of their lives, looking for lessons, strategies, and tactics that might help us today. Within each chapter, I also offer brief reflections on how their experiences illuminate present-day issues and, in the conclusion, consider nine specific characteristics that helped each woman become successful revolutionaries, even if their stories didn't always have happy endings. Some saw their comrades killed or their work undone, others went to an early grave, but the fire that animated their various struggles is nonetheless inspiring.

I also want to acknowledge that there have always been leftist women activists in the West who shared in similar struggles against capitalism. But, at least in the United States, socialist women activists found themselves subsumed under liberal feminist ideologies that upheld the capitalist status quo. With its focus on increasing professional opportunities for privileged women at the top of the income distribution, liberal feminism supports a worldview wherein everything is just fine as long as women have better access to wealth and power. Over a century ago, socialist women understood that the "bourgeois feminists" of the West showed little interest in the lives of working-class women. They imagined a political project that challenged the exploitation of unpaid labor in the private sphere as part of a wider program to overcome the injustices perpetuated by a free-market system that produces systemic forms of discrimination.

The historical context of tsarist and Soviet Russia as well as that of state socialist Bulgaria differs from the contemporary political landscapes of North America, the countries of Western Europe, and the nations of the Global South. The women profiled in these pages focused primarily on the tensions between gender and class identities, rather than on race, sexuality, ability, gender identity, or other categories of difference that animate present-day conversations about social justice and the need for progressive change. Tsarist autocracy, European fascism, and the savage immiseration produced by capitalism served as the primary targets of their theoretical and practical interventions. But this does not mean that their insights and experiences are irrelevant to us. Even if their historical and cultural contexts differed from our own, their

Elena Lagadinova and Angela Davis on Davis's visit to Bulgaria in 1972

victories and failures have in many ways helped to shape the world we have inherited today, both directly and indirectly.

When the American civil rights activist Angela Davis visited Elena Lagadinova in Bulgaria in 1972, for instance, Davis's goal was to highlight the incompatibility of American claims to upholding democratic freedoms with their poor record on civil rights. Persistent accusations from the Eastern Bloc about U.S. domestic racism played an important role in forcing political progress in the United States.[20] Rather than being intersectional, women like Angela Davis or Elena Lagadinova were *confluential* in their politics. Instead of focusing on the fixed points where different social identities or movements meet (that is their intersections), socialist women often viewed categories like race, class, and gender as distinct rivers flowing into each other from different tributaries, rivers which can mix and grow larger and more powerful. A familiarity with the wider history of socialist women's activism might inspire new ideas for strategic interventions in our contemporary political context.

Both the Western press and her own Bolshevik colleagues once referred to Alexandra Kollontai as a "Valkyrie" after the legendary female warriors of Norse mythology. I have adopted this word for my title because each of the women profiled in these pages, in their own way, fought like superhuman warriors to support causes that defined the twentieth century. Their personal stories reveal certain similar characteristics that they shared, characteristics that made them successful in their quests to create, further, and defend social change. To face the many challenges of the twenty-first century, we need a broader vision of emancipation that targets the forces that produce and exacerbate inequality at all levels of society.

The Red Valkyries can help show us the way.

1

The Sniperess

Lyudmila Pavlichenko (1916–1974)

In 1942, union members at the Colt Firearms Manufacturing Company in Hartford, Connecticut, gifted a young Soviet soldier a new automatic pistol and a bullet marked with the number 310. The famous Hollywood director Charlie Chaplin knelt before this same soldier and kissed each of the fingers of her right and left hands. The folk singer Woody Guthrie wrote a ballad in her honor, and a widowed millionaire proposed marriage. Lyudmila Pavlichenko was the first Soviet woman to be a guest at the White House; she became chums with Eleanor Roosevelt and stunned American audiences in forty-three states with her rousing speeches to whip up public support for the opening of a second front against the Axis in continental Europe. "Every German who remains alive will kill women, children, and old folks," she told a crowd of incredulous American journalists. "Dead Germans are harmless. Therefore, if I kill a German, I am saving lives."[1] When asked how she felt about shooting in cold blood the men she could see clearly through the sight on her rifle, she merely replied: "How can a human being feel when killing a poisonous snake?"[2]

When the Soviet military honored her for her 257th confirmed kill, Pavlichenko told her superiors, "I'll get more." And she kept her promise. Between the age of twenty-four and twenty-six, Pavlichenko officially racked up 309 confirmed kills, the highest tally of any woman sniper in history. The workers in Connecticut gave Pavlichenko the pistol and

A publicity still of Lyudmila Pavlichenko in 1942

the engraved bullet in hopes that she would use it to kill her 310th.

Born in 1916 in a town just outside of Kiev, Pavlichenko (née Belova) was the daughter of a factory worker and a teacher. Her father, Mikhail Ivanovich Belov, fought in World War I, joined the Bolsheviks during the Russian revolution, and defended the new workers' state with the Red Army during the civil war. Lyudmila's mother, Elena Trofimovna Belova, was a teacher of foreign languages, and taught her daughter to speak some English. The family settled in Kiev in 1932. When Lyudmila was "barely 15 years old," she fell for a boy and found herself pregnant.[3] She married at sixteen years old and took the Ukrainian name Pavlichenko, which she kept for the rest of her life. Lyudmila's mother looked after Lyudmila's son, Rostislav, so that Lyudmila could continue with her studies and her work in the Arsenal factory in Kiev, which manufactured armaments. Lyudmila and her husband soon divorced. Her unplanned pregnancy and the short-lived marriage left her with a healthy suspicion of men: "My limited but harsh life experience prompted me always to be on my guard with members of the opposite sex," she explains in her memoir, *Lady Death*.[4]

Pavlichenko went to a firing range for the first time after hearing a boy boast about his shooting abilities; there, she discovered her remarkable natural aptitude for marksmanship. In the Soviet Union of the 1930s, the ever-paranoid Stalin, fearing an impending invasion from the capitalist West, encouraged young people to pursue various military hobbies through an organization called the Society for the Assistance of Defense, Aircraft and Chemical Construction, which went by the acronym "Osoaviakhim." Despite Stalin having reversed the progressive policies of the early post-revolutionary period in 1936, making it harder for women to get divorced and outlawing abortion (which had been legalized in 1920), the Soviet government also urged women to enter what were then considered masculine professions, as the historian Anna Krylova has explored, despite their continuing "obligations" as mothers and wives.[5] Women in this era were able to train as pilots, parachutists, and snipers, proving to skeptical Soviet men and boys that women excelled in military fields that required extensive concentration, patience, and skill. Pavlichenko honed her shooting abilities with the support of these military clubs. In one instance, she competed in a tournament with twelve different prizes for twelve different feats of marksmanship and won them all.

After several years of work in the Arsenal factory, Pavlichenko decided to further her studies at the University of Kiev. In her memoir, she reports that she found herself enamored of the fields of anthropology, history, and foreign languages: "It soon became clear which were my favorite subjects: basic archeology and ethnography, history of the USSR, ancient history, Latin, and—given a choice of two foreign languages—English."[6] As she studied, she continued to perfect her shooting while raising her son and completed a special sniper training course within the Osoaviakhim, carefully saving all of the medals she won at various competitions.

Although Nazi Germany and the Soviet Union signed a non-aggression pact in 1939, Hitler invaded anyway. During his unexpected launch of Operation Barbarossa on June 22, 1941, the twenty-four-year-old Lyudmila Pavlichenko was in Odessa, conducting research for her thesis. Once war was declared, she learned that all those born between 1905 and 1918 were subject to conscription. Born in 1916, Pavlichenko decided to volunteer her services. She recalled: "My meeting with the enlistment office seemed to me to be a very formal one, and I put on my best crêpe-de-chine dress and some beautiful white high-heeled sandals. In my handbag I had my passport, student card and graduation certificate from Kiev's Osoaviakhim sniper school."[7] The enlistment officer tried to convince her that women were better off serving as nurses or medics in non-combatant roles, but Pavlichenko insisted that she should serve as a sniper on the front lines. When the officer resisted, she dumped her medals and official sniper training certificate onto the table in front of him. This was the Soviet Union, and anyone who was qualified, man or woman, could volunteer to sacrifice for the defense of the world's first workers' state. Seeing that the young woman in her "best crêpe-de-chine dress" and "white high-heeled sandals" would not be deterred, the recruiter duly enlisted the twenty-four-year-old mother into the Independent Maritime Army.

Lyudmila Pavlichenko numbered among the ranks of about 800,000 women who served in the Soviet armed forces during World War II, or about a million women if you include those who risked their lives as guerilla fighters with the partisans. Although the numbers are fuzzy, historians suggest that women made up about 3 percent of the Soviet military. Eighty of them would go on to become Heroes of the Soviet Union, the highest honor the state could bestow upon one of its citizens.

Perhaps the best-known Soviet front-line women combatants were the *Nachthexen* (Night Witches), the 588th Night Bomber Regiment, which later changed its name to the 46th Taman Guards Night Bomber Aviation Regiment. An aviator named Marina Raskova, known as the Soviet Amelia Earhart, used her personal connection with Stalin to convince him to approve the formation of three all-female aviation regiments to make use of the Soviet girls and women who had trained as pilots in the 1930s. A twenty-eight-year-old pilot named Yevdokiya Bershanskaya was chosen to lead the 588th. The regiment consisted of women between the ages of eighteen and twenty-six who flew outdated Polikarpov Po-2 biplanes made of plywood and canvas, which their fellow pilots called "sewing machines." These old crop dusters could only carry a few bombs for each run, so their pilots conducted as many as eighteen sorties in a night. Their flimsy construction meant that enemy fire easily damaged the biplanes, and since they flew at such low altitudes, their pilots and navigators lacked parachutes until 1944. Stealth provided their only advantage.

The biplane pilots flew in low, cut their engines, and glided over German targets to drop their bombs. Nazi soldiers on the ground only heard a soft whooshing sound before the devastating explosions, and they likened the *swoosh* of the biplanes to the sound of a witch's broom, hence the name *Nachthexen*. These bombing raids proved so successful at terrorizing the Germans that the Nazis apparently awarded an Iron Cross to any soldier who shot down a Polikarpov Po-2 biplane. Between 1941 and 1945, the Night Witches collectively flew over 23,000 sorties and dropped more than 3,000 tons of bombs on German targets. From the 588th/46th regiment alone, twenty-three female pilots earned the title "Hero of the Soviet Union."[8]

The Soviets also formed the 1077th Anti-Aircraft Regiment, which participated in the defense of Stalingrad in 1942. This regiment consisted entirely of ill-trained, ill-equipped teenage girls, many of whom lost their lives using their anti-aircraft guns against German Panzer tanks. The 1st Separate Volunteer Women's Rifle Brigade also mobilized Soviet women trained in marksmanship. Other famous Soviet female snipers include Roza Shanina, who kept a detailed war diary before her death in 1945, and the grandmother sniper, Nina Petrova, who volunteered to fight even though she was too old to be drafted. This middle-aged woman had a confirmed tally of 122 kills and trained an additional 512 snipers before her own death in the last year of the War. All together, the Soviet Union's female snipers sent over 11,000 Axis troops to their graves. Among the many Soviet women and girls who fought with the partisan resistance, the best known was a young woman named Zoya Kosmodemyanskaya, whom the Germans captured. Although brutally tortured, she died without divulging the names of her comrades in arms. Pavlichenko was just one of the many Soviet women fighting in what the Russians still call "The Great Patriotic War," but she remains the best known because of her travels in the West. Soviet propagandists elevated her as a role model of valor and perseverance in hopes of inspiring other Soviet youth to follow in her footsteps.

After her enlistment, Pavlichenko joined the Second Company of the Second Battalion in the 54th Stepan Razin Rifle Regiment of the 25th "V.I. Chapayev" Division of the Independent Maritime Army. Pavlichenko traded her feminine attire for an ill-fitting, oversized male uniform. Due to equipment shortages, her superior officers sent the accomplished sniper into battle with nothing more than a hand grenade. She would not get her first rifle until the second half of July 1941 when a comrade in arms was injured and bequeathed her his standard Mosin rifle 1891/1939 model. Shortly thereafter, the 54th regiment was resupplied and Pavlichenko acquired a brand-new Mosin rifle with the factory grease still on it. On August 8, 1941, in Belyayevka, Pavlichenko opened her sniper's tally with the killing of two Romanians in rapid succession on the same day that the siege of Odessa began.

Pavlichenko fought with the 54th rifle regiment to repel the Nazi-allied Romanian troops trying to break through into Odessa from the south. But after only eleven days on the front lines, picking off enemy soldiers through her telescopic sight, Pavlichenko sustained the first of her four injuries in the field when a mortar shell hit two meters from her. "The shock wave smashed my beloved rifle to smithereens, threw me backwards in the bottom of a trench and covered me with earth," she recalls in her memoir. "I came to in the hospital: my regimental mates had dug me out and taken me to Odessa along with other wounded and shell-shocked Red Army soldiers of the first battalion."[9] After convalescing in the rear, Pavlichenko returned to duty on the front and received her first promotion to corporal. She continued to snipe the enemy soldiers, and, by September 1941, was promoted to junior sergeant. For her hundredth kill, her superiors gave her a specially engraved SVT-40 rifle with a PU telescopic sight.[10]

In mid-October, Lyudmila sustained her second injury when a mortar splinter hit above her left eye. Bleeding heavily and losing consciousness, a female medical orderly pulled Pavlichenko from the front and managed to rush her back to the medical battalion. At the triage station, the orderly pointed to the special engraving on Pavlichenko's rifle that acknowledged her 100 confirmed kills and insisted that she be treated at once. Impressed by her tally, the doctors agreed to operate on Pavlichenko immediately, saving her life a second time.

But defending Odessa was a lost cause, and Pavlichenko was still convalescing when the order came down to abandon the city for Sevastopol. Despite her success as a sniper, some of her male comrades refused to give women like Pavlichenko the respect they deserved. On the boat evacuating her from Odessa, Pavlichenko fell into conversation with a sailor who opined that war was no place for women. She had heard this sentiment expressed many times before but refused to let it undermine her determination to fight:

> I had neither the time nor the desire to argue with the navigator. During the dreadful war, in which our people were fighting for their very survival, everyone who was confident in military knowledge and skills, regardless of his or her sex or national affiliation, had to join the ranks and make whatever contribution they were capable of to wipe out the German Fascist invaders. Only then would we be able to defeat the enemy.[11]

Once she was established in Sevastopol, Pavlichenko's superiors promoted her to senior sergeant on November 4, 1941, and gave her the command of a mixed-sex sniper platoon, where she again encountered resistance from Soviet men who initially had trouble taking orders from a woman. As part of her promotion, Pavlichenko acquired a new winter uniform with a Tula-Tokarev (TT) pistol. For the remainder of her combat service, she never went into battle without this pistol and a hand grenade. She understood that the Nazis would show no mercy if they captured her alive: "Neither the Russians nor the Germans took snipers prisoner but shot them directly on the spot. For women there was another variation – death preceded by gang rape. Therefore, the grenade was for rolling under the enemy's feet, seven bullets from the TT were for anyone who came too close, and the eighth was for yourself."[12]

The Nazis committed horrific atrocities on the Eastern Front. Hitler viewed the east as a future *Lebensraum* for ethnic Aryans, and invading German soldiers murdered civilians and burned villages to the ground. For women in combat positions, recurring memories of the violence haunted them for the rest of their lives. Nobel Prize–winning oral historian

Svetlana Alexievich captured the brutal reality of life for Soviet women in her moving book *The Unwomanly Face of War*. One woman she interviewed recalled the gruesome torture and death of a comrade. "One of our nurses was captured ... A day later we took back that village ... We found her: eyes put out, breasts cut off. They had impaled her on a stake ... It was freezing cold, and she was white as could be, and her hair was all gray ... She was nineteen years old."[13] In an article addressed to American readers, Pavlichenko also painted a vivid picture of the shocking violence of the German troops on the Eastern Front:

> I do not believe the American people as a whole entirely understand what war is like. Most of you so far only feel it as an inconvenience—doing without gasoline, being a little limited in the amount of sugar you use. You do not know what it is to have bombs falling all around you. You do not know what it is to see babies murdered, women and girls ravished by the Hitlerite beasts. You do not know what it is to find the charred bodies of your own comrades burned and tortured beyond recognition, to see rows of brave, fine people—people you knew —hanging along the roadside. You do not know what it is to walk into a home for old people won back from the Germans, as I did on the Sovkhoz Ilyichka, near Odessa. It was early morning, and the sun was just rising, and we went in to set the people there free. But what we found were the bodies of 108 old people, shot and tortured, slashed to pieces, blown up by grenades. 108 people, all of them old and ill. And so depraved are those Hitlerites that the old women had all been raped.[14]

In addition to the threat of rape, torture, and death at the hands of the Germans, Soviet women in the military also faced pervasive sexism and harassment perpetrated by men on their own side. In one case, a brigade of sniper women in the 715th regiment returned from the front lines to find an order that they mop the floors of the headquarters. "No

Way! was their unequivocal response: that was work for soldiers on fatigue duties. What did this commandant take them for?"[15] For their disobedience, the brigade spent the night in the guardhouse as punishment, but the women from the field kitchens apparently rewarded them with better meals, in solidarity. In another case, a group of snipers came back to their dugout after forty-eight hours of intense fighting without sleep. A courier appeared and told the deputy platoon commander to send two women to wash the floors of the officer's quarters. Even though these snipers had fought on the front lines side by side with their male comrades, the officers still considered cleaning to be women's work. This deputy platoon commander also refused the order. For her disobedience, she was sentenced to five days in the guardhouse until a more senior officer reversed her sentence and sent her back to the dugout to get some sleep.[16]

Sexual harassment and the fear of assault also haunted the Soviet women soldiers. "Amorous" Soviet men sometimes attacked their female comrades, and the women developed various strategies to protect themselves.[17] Pavlichenko herself admitted that she preferred fighting on the front lines in part because of uncomfortable situations with men of higher ranks back in the camp:

> I am not giving away any secrets if I say that serving as a woman in the army has its particular challenges. One's behavior in male company must be even-handed, strict, and beyond reproach; no flirting with anyone, ever! But life takes its own course and there were times when difficulties arose. They were not created at all by rank-and-file soldiers, but rather by my "comrade-officers," using both their status as commanders and the clause in the military code that a commanding officer's order must be fulfilled and one must answer for failure to do so in accordance to wartime laws. We called this "taking a fancy to." That is why I preferred to spend more time on the front

line, albeit under enemy fire. Here the chances of catching the eye of some amorous possessor of three or four little cubes or bars on his collar tabs (that is, from the middle and senior officer corps) remained minimal.[18]

Pavlichenko did not avoid her male comrades in arms completely. In Sevastopol, this Valkyrie met and fell in love with a "Viking," Alexei Kitsenko, whom she described as a "big, well-proportioned, blue-eyed and blond-haired" officer. On December 19, 1941, a shell fragment lodged itself in Pavlichenko's back. She collapsed, bleeding profusely into the earth and believing her time had come. Under heavy fire, Kitsenko found Pavlichenko half dead and carried her to safety at great risk to his own life. When she had healed from her third serious injury, Kitsenko declared his love, and they were formally married at the front.

Pavlichenko's relationship with Kitsenko, a fellow sniper, gave her strength at a time of relentless bad news. The Red Army was taking heavy losses and had retreated from vast swaths of western territory now occupied by the Nazis, and demoralization began to set in among the troops. The Soviet authorities needed to propagate inspiring stories of heroism in the face of the never-ending Nazi onslaught; the accomplishments of the young and photogenic Pavlichenko, her skills as a counter-sniper (a sniper who hunts enemy snipers), her bravery as a soldier, and her rapid rise through the ranks perfectly suited their needs. In January of 1942, while Pavlichenko was still recuperating from her back injury, a cadre of journalists and photographers visited her; they posed her for photos with her rifle and creatively embellished her life story to make it sound even more heroic. "Journalistic invention is just one component of propaganda," Pavlichenko wrote. "People need a living hero to make things more convincing. It seemed that I had been chosen for this role in the coastal army's political department."[19] Between 1942 and 1945, the

Soviets dropped over 100,000 leaflets on the German–Soviet front lines featuring Pavlichenko's portrait, a brief biography of her accomplishments, and the words "Shoot the enemy and don't miss!"[20] Lyudmila Pavlichenko became a household name in the Soviet Union and inspired many young men and women to sign up for sniper training schools. Even the Germans came to know her name, alternately trying to lure her over to their side with promises of chocolates and promotions and threatening to chop her into 309 pieces if they captured her.

During the winter of 1941–2, Pavlichenko found herself both famous and madly in love. She often went sniping (or what they called "hunting") with Kitsenko and together they terrorized the enemy troops surrounding Sevastopol. In her "Viking," this Red Valkyrie found a sympathetic equal: "As a husband, he was always concerned for me and protected me from various adversaries as far as that was possible on the front line."[21] She embraced the hyperreal blur of war and, despite the death and destruction, enjoyed the utter conviction that her cause was just as the Germans had invaded the Soviet Union. Pavlichenko's training and aptitude allowed her to defend a country she loved and she shared this overarching purpose not only with a fellow sniper, but also with a comrade she adored. "With him I felt for the first time the meaning of love, requited and all-consuming love, and I was completely happy in those days."[22]

But during the infamous Siege of Sevastopol in 1942, Pavlichenko suffered a fourth wound, which ended her service on the front lines. In her memoir, she describes the circumstances of that fateful day:

> On the morning of 3 March 1942 the weather was so fine and warm that it was impossible to stay in the dugout. Alexei and I decided to breakfast in the fresh air—to the chirping of the irrepressible Sevastopol sparrows. With his arm around my

Alexei Kitsenko and Lyudmila Pavlichenko in 1942

shoulders, my husband was sitting beside me on a fallen tree and relating some humorous incident from his childhood. The enemy artillery attack on the lines of the 54th regiment started suddenly. It came from a long-range ordinance. The first shells exploded far in the rear, and the second salvo fell short, but the third ... "You're not tired, are you?" Kitsenko had just asked me when the third shell exploded behind our backs. Dozens of splinters whistled through the air. My junior lieutenant shielded me from them, but did not escape wounds himself. In the first minute I did not think it was serious. Alexei clutched his right shoulder and groaned. But then the blood streamed profusely down the sleeve of his tunic, his arm hung limp, and a pallor began to cover his face.[23]

Pavlichenko rushed her husband to the field hospital where they operated on his arm: a lot of blood lost, the wound serious. She asked for, and was granted, leave from the front to remain by his side. Years later, Pavlichenko recounted her thoughts as she waited for Kitsenko to recover. "I reflected on many things, recalling my first meeting with him, the forest at sunset, when the junior lieutenant had found me under the shattered tree, his declaration of love, and our happy conjugal life. There was no one closer or dearer to me than Alexei Arkadyevich. He had remained cheerful in difficult circumstances,

did not despair at failure, and success did not go to his head ...
I trusted him more than I trusted myself."[24] During the night,
Kitsenko struggled for consciousness, his confusion and delir-
ium interrupted by brief moments of lucidity when he tried
to be optimistic. But his wound was too severe. On March 4,
1942, the "Viking" died in Lyudmila Pavlichenko's arms.

After three sleepless nights in their dugout home, Pavlichenko, believing herself uninjured, finally picked up her rifle
to go hunting. Her arms trembled so violently that she could
not hold the weapon steady enough to aim. When the shaking
continued, she sought out a neuropathologist in the medical
battalion who diagnosed her with shell shock. She left the
front lines for medical treatment, but she never fought as a
sniper again. The Soviets faced a crushing defeat at Sevastopol, and her superiors found a different way to make use of
Pavlichenko's talents.

After being reassigned to Moscow in August 1942, Pavlichenko found herself in the Kremlin standing with two other
young Soviets in front of Joseph Stalin himself, the man who
had purged his own experienced Party comrades throughout
the late 1930s, leaving him ill-prepared to fight a war against
Nazi Germany. The American first lady Eleanor Roosevelt was
planning an International Student Assembly in Washington,
DC, and Pavlichenko had been chosen as the Soviet delegation's sole female member. Always the disciplined soldier, she
accepted this assignment without question. Before leaving
Moscow, the three young "students" found themselves in a
secret storeroom being equipped with new clothes and luxury
items almost unknown in the USSR at the time. Stalin asked
them if they needed anything else for their journey, but the
three young Soviets stood in silent awe. Finally, Pavlichenko
worked up the nerve to ask Stalin for a Russian–English dictionary and some English grammar books, which he gave her.
Pavlichenko wanted to brush up on her language skills before

embarking on what seemed like a sudden and out-of-the-blue journey halfway across the world.

On August 23, 1942, the Nazis launched an all-out offensive to take Stalingrad, resulting in one of the bloodiest battles in history. The Soviet Union desperately needed the British and the Americans, its official allies, to launch attacks that would force Hitler to recommit troops away from the Eastern Front, but although Allied troops fought in North Africa and the British bombed the Germans and supported the partisan resistance in countries such as Greece, Yugoslavia, Bulgaria, and Hungary, neither country would commit to opening a second European front. It was only after the Soviets repelled the Germans at Stalingrad in February 1943 that the tide of the war began to turn—the Sicilian landings took place in July 1943 and the storming of the beaches of Normandy in June 1944.

The Soviet delegation spent their first night in the United States as the personal guests of the Roosevelts, the first citizens of their country to stay in the White House. From Washington, Pavlichenko and her fellow "students"—Vladimir Pchelintsev, a twenty-three-year-old sniper and Hero of the Soviet Union, and Nikolai Krasavchenko, leader of the Moscow youth organization—began their four-month international tour of the United States, Canada, and the United Kingdom between August and December 1942, during which months the world's newspapers brimmed with stories about the heavy fighting around Stalingrad. The delegation's goal was a simple one: to raise funds for the Soviet war effort and to sway public opinion in favor of a second European front. But from the moment they set foot in the American capital, all attention focused on Pavlichenko. The American press marveled at the fresh-faced twenty-six-year-old sniper with 309 fascist kills. Americans could not reconcile the visage of this young woman with the role of a cold-blooded sniper. Her youth, health, and natural good looks fascinated the American public.

The questions she received from American journalists focused far more on her appearance than on her heroic accomplishments. In his own recollections of their time in the United States, her fellow sniper Pchelintsev recalled that "the trickiest, and sometimes downright impertinent, questions were directed toward Pavlichenko. There were no bounds to the journalistic fraternity's curiosity."[25] When the *New York Times* reported that Pavlichenko wore "no lip rouge or make-up of any kind,"[26] a female journalist felt compelled to ask her whether girls fighting in Russia were allowed to wear makeup at the front. Pavlichenko simply replied, "There is no rule against it, but who has time to think of her shiny nose when a battle is going on?"[27] In her memoir, she reprints a verbatim transcript of a typical press conference:

Question (from a woman journalist): Is that your parade uniform or your everyday uniform?
Answer: We have no time for parades at the moment.
Question (also from a woman): But the uniform makes you look fat. Or don't you mind?
Answer: I am proud to wear the uniform of the legendary Red Army. It has been sanctified by the blood of my comrades who have fallen in combat with the Fascists. It bears the order of Lenin, an award for military distinction. I wish you could experience a bombing raid. Honestly, you would immediately forget about the cut of your outfit.
Question: The tobacco company Phillip Morris is offering you a contract. They are ready to pay half a million dollars to put your portrait on cigarette packets. Will you agree to it?
Answer: No. They can go to the devil.[28]

Writing in the "Features for Modern Women" section of the *Philadelphia Inquirer*, journalist Ruth Cowan enthused over Pavlichenko's appearance:

Men wanted to meet her—this attractive 26-year-old Kiev University student who set out to be a history scholar and has now become a modern military legend. Men in uniform accepted her ... Girls crowded around, too. One wanted to know "How does she keep that beautiful complexion?" Liudmila has that rosy-cheeked, healthy look that mothers claim carrot-eating will give. One slim co-ed said: "I wish she would take me back to Russia and teach me to be a sniper."[29]

Americans simply could not reconcile their stereotypes of what was "womanly" with Pavlichenko's exploits as a sniper. When Pavlichenko visited Boston, for example, a reporter for the *Christian Science Monitor* observed: "Those expecting the stalwart girl sniper to be callous and hardened as the result of her experiences were amazed to greet a thoroughly warm and human personality. Lieutenant Pavlichenko, who wears four wound stripes on her sleeve and four medals upon her chest,

A portrait of Lyudmila Pavlichenko in 1942

is vigorous and straightforward in manner, but at the same time thoroughly feminine."[30] In his song "Miss Pavilichenko" (*sic.*), Woody Guthrie highlighted the contrast between Pavlichenko's "sweet face" and the "more than three hundred Nazi-dogs" that fell by her gun.[31]

In a radio interview with Alice Hughes, Pavlichenko complained about the "silly questions" journalists asked her in America.[32] "It is plain to see that with American women what is important is whether they wear silk underwear under their uniforms," she said. "What the uniform stands for, they have yet to learn."[33] These comments about the frivolity of American women did not go unchallenged. In her "The Gentler Sex" column in the *Washington Post*, Malvina Livesay defended American women and suggested that the comments about Pavlichenko's underwear were the result of her being in a country with "free speech, free press, and free laughter," a not-so-subtle dig at the authoritarian restrictions of Stalin's Soviet Union. Livesay also felt compelled to suggest that there was something unwomanly about Pavlichenko's lack of interest in her own appearance. "What if American women are concerned about the looks of their uniforms? And even the underwear underneath?" Livesay opined. "Isn't it a part of military philosophy that an efficient warrior takes pride in his appearance? ... Isn't Joan of Arc always pictured in beautiful and shining armor? ... Women the world over, for centuries, have retained their interest in self-adornment, and putting them into uniforms cannot stifle such interest overnight."[34] The early criticisms of her femininity must have bothered Pavlichenko, because she arrived at the International Student Assembly with her nails painted and her nose powdered.

After the Student Assembly, Pavlichenko and the Soviet delegation embarked on their tour of the United States. Pchelintsev and Krasavchenko spoke in one group of cities while First Lady Eleanor Roosevelt and Pavlichenko held events in another. Pavlichenko and Roosevelt grew close during their travels together. Pavlichenko also discovered her natural aptitude for public speaking. In Chicago, she shocked a room full of male journalists when she told them: "Gentlemen, I am 25 years old and I have killed 309 fascist occupants by now. Don't you think, gentlemen, that you have been hiding behind my back for too long?"[35] At first, the room remained quiet as her words sunk in, but then the men erupted in wild applause at the gutsy words of the sniper girl in her ill-fitting uniform. She later explained that she "wanted to think of something that would get through to them, to the fortunate, relaxed and extraordinarily calculating residents of the continent discovered by Columbus."[36] She had used the American obsession with her outward displays of femininity to her advantage, implying that American men were not man enough to fight against the Nazis as she did.

Throughout her tour of the United States, Pavlichenko collected many gifts and won accolades from various admirers.

Vladimir Pchelintsev, Nikolai Krasavchenko,
and Lyudmila Pavlichenko in 1942

On September 16, 1942, in front of an audience of 5,000 enthusiastic New Yorkers, the International Fur and Leather Workers Union presented Pavlichenko's male colleagues with two practical fleece-lined leather jackets but gave Pavlichenko what the *New York Times* described as "a full-length racoon coat of beautifully blended skins, which would be resplendent in an opera setting," as if the Red Army sniper would be attending the opera anytime soon.[37] The constant attention to her femininity wore on Pavlichenko, who complained to Eleanor Roosevelt, "In your country I feel like the butt of jokes, the object of idle curiosity, something like a circus act. Like a bearded woman. But I am an officer of the Red Army. I have fought and will go on fighting for the freedom and independence of my country."[38]

In her travels, Lyudmila Pavlichenko made many observations about life in the United States and found disturbing contradictions: "America itself is, on the one hand, a land of luxury, and, on the other, a land of destitution. The Negroes there live very badly. We had occasion to visit areas where basic living conditions were lacking. I was also surprised at the racial segregation: on the train there are special carriages—for Whites only, and for Coloureds only."[39] For Pavlichenko, the idea that the United States, supposedly a land of freedom and a champion of democracy, would divide people based on the color of their skin seemed incongruous. Pavlichenko's reflections on the segregation of American trains in 1942 reveals her sensitivity to the racialized disparities which thrived within a capitalist society.

Pavlichenko also noticed the inferior position of women in the United States, and she used her celebrity to try to educate American women on the egalitarianism possible under the socialist system:

Our women were on a basis of complete equality long before the war. From the first day of the Revolution full rights were granted the women of Soviet Russia. One of the most important things is that every woman has her own specialty. That is what actually makes them as independent as men. Soviet women have complete self-respect, because their dignity as human beings is fully recognized. Whatever we do, we are honored not just as women, but as individual personalities, as human beings. That is a very big word. Because we can be fully that, we feel no limitations because of our sex. That is why women have so naturally taken their places beside men in this war ... It seems strange to many Americans that women go into battle. They seem to think the war has changed them into some strange kind of creature between a man and a woman. But we are still feminine beings. We can still wear nice clothes and have polished fingernails in the proper time and place. We remain women and human beings as before. The war has made us tougher, that's all.[40]

Long before scholars such as Esther Newton and Judith Butler theorized gender performativity, Pavlichenko explained to her American readers that the traits that they considered masculine and feminine were not natural and fixed but rather situational and fluid.[41] Pavlichenko felt that socialism in the Soviet Union allowed citizens to be first and foremost "individual personalities" before they were men or women, and therefore nothing about their sex prevented them from pursuing goals that they wanted to pursue, even if those goals contradicted gender stereotypes. Pavlichenko simply could not understand why Americans thought that Soviet women who fought to defend their country lost any of their femininity, as both masculinity and femininity were fundamentally irrelevant to the goal of killing Nazis. Pavlichenko hadn't rejected the idea of powdering her nose in her response to the question about wearing makeup at the front, but simply

*Justice Robert Jackson, Lyudmila
Pavlichenko, and Eleanor Roosevelt*

asserted that there wasn't enough time in the middle of a battle. She believed in an ideal of femininity that could and should expand to include whatever it was that a woman wanted to do, even if that meant killing enemy combatants in cold blood.

This embrace of the "thoroughly feminine" by many socialist women's activists of the twentieth century often put them at odds with those Western feminists who wanted to erase or ignore gender distinctions, for some of whom true sexual equality lay in androgyny or other non-binary identities that rejected both poles of the gender stereotype spectrum. Early socialists, however, were less vexed by culturally specific ideals of masculinity and femininity. An excellent example of this is Stanislav Rostotsky's 1972 film, *The Dawns Here Are Quiet,* which valorizes the bravery of a group of female anti-aircraft gunners during World War II.[42] The protagonist of the film, Senior Sergeant Fedot Vaskov, commands the women and slowly grows to appreciate their courage and tenacity. The gunners are all classically beautiful, with one character wearing a silk slip under her ill-fitting uniform (perhaps a reference to the Americans' questions about Pavlichenko's preference for underwear). Throughout the largely black-and-white film, each of the female soldiers has weird technicolor dreams about love, family, or motherhood, further emphasizing their womanliness for the viewer and thereby blending standard tropes of femininity with military heroism.[43]

The Russian historian Anna Krylova argues that Soviet ideas about the gender binary during the late 1930s and early 1940s contained "diverse and contradictory dimensions." In Krylova's assessment, Western historians who argue that traditional gender roles were emphasized during the post-1936 era do so without also acknowledging the ways that many Soviet women at this time experienced real changes in their gendered subjectivity. Unlike in the West, where societies were obsessed with supposedly "natural" gender difference, Krylova argues, individual choices about gender performance in the Soviet Union mattered less than the collective political goal of building communism or defending the nation against Nazi invaders. Pavlichenko could have her face painted and kill Nazis, too.

By the late 1930s, women like Lyudmila Pavlichenko embraced what Krylova calls an "alternative femininity" that allowed both "maternal love and military violence" to coexist in a new ideal of Soviet womanhood. This created a "generation of professionally violent women-fighters."[44] Contrast the Soviet view with the laws embodied in the United States' Women's Armed Forced Integration Act of 1948, which limited the number of women that could serve in the American Air Force, Army and Navy to 2 percent of the total force. This act also prevented women from serving in combat positions or on vessels or aircraft that might see active combat (except hospital ships) and, with the exception of medical fields, placed a cap on the highest rank women could achieve. During Congressional testimony before the House Armed Services Committee in 1987, one national security expert explained that "in 1948, some in Congress believed that combat required physical strength that women did not possess. In addition, women's role in society was such that a policy of having women in combat was almost unthinkable."[45]

When Pavlichenko painted her nails, performing her femininity while also performing the identity of a battle-hardened soldier fresh from the front lines, she highlighted a key difference between US and Soviet approaches to gender. Both the Americans and the Soviets accepted patriarchal notions of a fixed gender binary. But where the Americans believed it "unthinkable" that women could serve in combat positions because they were weak, the Soviets trained them for combat positions that did not require specific upper body strength (such as snipers, pilots, parachutists, and anti-aircraft gunners). Rather than de-gendering the category of "soldier," Pavlichenko and women like her helped to create an idealized feminine version of it, something most liberal feminists would reject as problematically essentializing. Although Soviet policies may have reinforced stereotypes about the differences between men and women and could not erase the persistence of sexism, in the end, women in the Red Army progressed further and faster than their counterparts in the United States, who only achieved full combat parity with men in 2015.

After the Soviet Delegation left the United States, Pavlichenko and her two comrades visited Canada and the United Kingdom for more speeches, rallies, and press conferences. During all of their public engagements, Pavlichenko remained the center of attention. In London, she spoke to 2,000 women in November 1942. They presented her with a revolver to kill more Nazis, two English books for her studies at the University of Kiev, and a silver teapot for her future domestic life. The *New York Times* reported that "the stalwart Russian heroine" had "made a great impression" on the women of the UK.[46] Pchelintsev confirmed, "I have to say honestly that she was quite good with people. Guests and hosts were very taken by her smile and unaffectedness. Nikolai and I were no match for her."[47] While in Great Britain, Pavlichenko was appalled to learn that British women doing the same work as men did not earn the same wages, and she ached to return home. Her international tour ended in December 1942.

For her service, her government honored her as a Hero of the Soviet Union in 1943. Pavlichenko received a promotion to the rank of major and taught at a sniper school until 1944, when she applied for leave to finish her university degree in history. After the Allied victory, she officially worked as a journalist and military historian. In reality, Pavlichenko became a professional hero, polished up and trotted out for special occasions. The government celebrated and idolized her whenever Soviet citizens needed reminding of their triumph in the Great Patriotic War. Posters of Pavlichenko and her sniper's rifle made their way onto the bedroom walls of girls in India and China. When women took up arms as part of revolutionary struggles in countries such as Cuba, Vietnam, or Mozambique, they did so in the spirit of Pavlichenko and the other Soviet heroines of World War II.

More than twenty-four million Soviet people died in World War II, the highest toll of any country by far,[48] and the memory politics of the conflict have always been complicated by their use in bolstering Soviet, and later Russian, patriotism.[49] Because of the propaganda leaflets bearing her portrait, the wild embellishments of her life story in the Soviet Union, and the success of her American tour, some scholars have suggested that Pavlichenko was a fraud and her achievements a mere fabrication of the Soviet authorities.[50] But no one disputes that she volunteered to be a sniper or that she fought on the front lines. Military records confirm that she achieved the ranks of lieutenant in the Army and of major in the Navy, as well as her four injuries, the death of her husband, and her diagnosis with post-traumatic stress disorder. And it is certainly true that the privilege of traveling to the West kept her off the front lines after March 1942, and that unlike many women who returned from the front prematurely aged, with gray hair and various disabilities and disfigurements,

Pavlichenko's wounds had left only a small scar above her left eyebrow and a deeper scar on her back, which could be easily covered with clothing. Still, Pavlichenko witnessed the absolute horrors of German savagery on the Eastern Front and experienced firsthand the destruction wrought in the battles for Odessa and Sevastopol; she was twenty-four years old when she enlisted and just twenty-six when she traveled to the United States.

Pavlichenko also never fully recovered from the traumas of war and the loss of her "Viking." Like so many other women who fought on the front lines in the Soviet Union, Pavlichenko suffered survivor's guilt, depression, and post-traumatic stress. "My wounds from the front and shell shock played up more and more as the years went by."[51] She formally retired from the military in 1953 as an "invalid, second class." When Eleanor Roosevelt came to the Soviet Union in 1957 and visited her old friend, Pavlichenko was living in a humble two-room apartment in Moscow.

Roosevelt's friendship with Pavlichenko may have inspired the former first lady in profound and interesting ways. She became the chair of the First Presidential Commission on the Status of Women in 1961, appointed by President John F. Kennedy, who had seen the Soviets invest so much in the education and training of their women and became convinced that the development of American women's talents was essential for the national security of the United States. In the last public position of her life, Roosevelt oversaw the review of 421 pieces of legislation regarding women until her death in November 1962. The 1963 report "American Women" outlined specific ways that American laws and workplaces discriminated against women, and its recommendations set the stage for the birth of the "second wave" feminist movement. Pavlichenko's visit to the United States and her friendship with Eleanor Roosevelt may have played an important role in confirming for the former first lady that her country needed to provide its own women with opportunities outside of the narrow confines of marriage and motherhood.

Pavlichenko titled the final chapter of her memoir "I Am Sidelined!" With the advent of the nuclear age, she mourned the loss of the sniper's art and feared that another world war would destroy all humanity. Knowing that the next global conflagration would involve intercontinental ballistic missiles rather than front-line combat, Pavlichenko watched as her expertise and experience became obsolete. Pavlichenko still retains her title as the woman sniper with the highest tally in history, largely because no one has had the chance to beat her. At the end of her memoir, Pavlichenko recounts sitting alone in the "majestic silence" of the Fraternal Cemetery in Sevastopol:

> Just the cheeping of the birds fluttering between the cedars. Just the gusts of wind which occasionally blew in from the sea and rustled the thickets of wild rose. Just the crystal-clear vault of the heavens gleaming over the paths, trails and gravestones of the soldiers' memorial separated from the world by a tall, solid wall. Nothing has changed here since the time when the troops and officers of the 54th Rifle regiment buried Junior Lieutenant Alexei Kitsenko, a valiant officer and my husband.[52]

As with so many veterans, Pavlichenko self-medicated with alcohol, and sank deeper into depression. On October 10, 1974, at the age of fifty-eight, Lyudmila Pavlichenko died of a stroke in her grown son's arms. Two years later, the Soviets immortalized her on a commemorative stamp. To this day, variations of, and embellishments on, her life story continue to circulate on websites such as RejectedPrincesses.com, in comedy series such as *Drunk History*, and in films such as *Battle for Sevastopol*, a Russian–Ukrainian co-production made before the Russian annexation of Crimea in 2014.[53] The sniperess still fascinates.

There is a wonderful anecdote from Svetlana Alexievich's book about Soviet women in World War II. At the time of the Cuban Missile Crisis in October 1962, a female veteran was preparing for a holiday at a seaside resort. Among her clothes and toiletries, she decided to pack her army card in case a new war broke out. "I was already on the seashore, resting, and I happened to tell someone at the table in the dining room that, in preparing to come here, I took along my army card," the veteran explained to Alexievich. "But a man at our table got all excited: 'No, only a Russian woman can take her army card with her as she leaves for a resort, and think that if anything happens she'll go straight to the recruiting office.'"[54]

Exactly how did it come to pass that *only a Russian woman* could do this in 1962? To understand the world that Lyudmila Pavlichenko and her fellow veterans were born into, we have to go back in time. There, we will meet a troika of Red Valkyries who helped make the Bolshevik revolution and build the world's first workers' state. Each in their own way laid the foundations for a unique form of socialist women's activism that transformed the lives of hundreds of millions of women in the twentieth century, including that of Lyudmila Pavlichenko. Of these, none was more prominent and controversial than the original "Communist Valkyrie": Alexandra Mikhailovna Kollontai.

2
The Communist Valkyrie
Alexandra Kollontai (1872–1952)

Portrait of Alexandra Kollontai

The American press obsessed over her. They called her the "Red Rose of the Revolution," the "Jeanne d'Arc of the Proletariat," the "Heroine of the Bolsheviki upheaval in Petrograd," and the "Proletarian Siren." In 1918, *Current Opinion* announced to its incredulous readers that "she holds a cabinet portfolio, dresses like a Parisian, and does not believe in marriage."[1] In 1924, the *Philadelphia Inquirer* dubbed her the "Communist Valkyrie," and a year later, the *New York Times* made the salacious accusation that she was arranging fake marriages to promote "red propaganda" in Norway, where she served as a diplomat. In 1927, the *Washington Post* revealed that the new Soviet ambassador to Mexico—"who has had six husbands" —had been refused entry into the United States because the government considered her a threat to public safety.

Although socialist, communist, and anarchist women had been fighting for the emancipation of women since the mid-nineteenth century, none of them had the practical power, platform, and lasting international influence of Alexandra Mikhailovna Kollontai. From our vantage point in the twenty-first century, Kollontai's prescience is astounding given that she theorized, agitated, and organized for women over a hundred years ago. She fought for women's full emancipation and concomitantly reimagined the roles of love, sex, friendship, and family in a future socialist society, while also living out that reimagination within the constraints of fin de siècle Russia. As a left-fluid individual, Kollontai started her political life as a pacifist and social democrat, became a revolutionary communist, and then flirted briefly with anarchism before being sent off to exile as one of the world's first women ambassadors.

Her courageous sex positivity attempted to liberate women from the suffocating strictures of Victorian morality. As historian Maria Bucur writes in her book *The Century of Women*:

> More than any other communist revolutionary in imperial Russia, Kollontai developed an original analysis of gender

inequality and proposed the ideology of free love—doing away with the institution of marriage and parenting as they had been solidified through law and practice, to pave the way for a new form of equality and new types of communal loyalties ... She envisioned a world in which any person could grow up to the full potential of his or her abilities, so that all would be ready to dedicate themselves to the common good without unequal burdens placed on their shoulders by virtue of their gender.[2]

While some of Kollontai's ideas might seem anachronistic to us, others still feel as radical today as they did in 1922.

Born in Saint Petersburg in 1872, Alexandra Mikhailovna Domontovich hailed from a wealthy but politically liberal aristocratic family. Her father served as a general in the tsar's army. Her mother was the daughter of a wealthy Finnish businessman; she had fled a miserable arranged marriage to be with Alexandra's father, causing quite the scandal in their social circles at the time. Educated at home by a private governess, the young Alexandra proved an eager pupil and craved knowledge. By age seven, she could already converse comfortably in French, German, and English as well as Finnish, Italian, and Bulgarian, and had a good knowledge of Ukrainian. "My childhood was a very happy one, judging by outward circumstances." Kollontai reported in her 1926 autobiography. "I was the youngest, the most spoiled, and the most coddled member of the family."[3] When her father was sent to the Balkans to help write a constitution for a Bulgarian state newly liberated from the Ottoman Empire in 1878, his precocious daughter accompanied him and got her first taste of political freedom born of revolutionary struggle.

Given the realities of life for women in her social class, however, Kollontai's future depended on finding an appropriate husband. "I was supposed to make a good match and mother was bent upon marrying me off at a very early age. My oldest sister, at the age of nineteen, had contracted marriage with a highly placed gentleman who was nearly seventy. I revolted against this marriage of convenience, this marriage for money and wanted to marry only for love, out of a great passion."[4] At the age of twenty-one, over her mother's fierce objections, she married a poor cousin, Vladimir Kollontai, took his name, and gave birth to a son, Mikhail (Misha), in 1893.

Kollontai soon found it impossible to settle into a traditional married life. Although born into privilege, she could not ignore the turbulent politics of tsarist Russia at the time. The Emancipation Reform of 1861 had freed the serfs from their feudal masters and the rise of industrial capitalism challenged the autocratic rule of the Romanov Dynasty. Liberated peasants flocked to the urban areas, and Saint Petersburg and other cities teemed with former serfs with nothing to sell but their labor. The social upheavals of the late nineteenth century and the growing influence of Marxism across Europe inspired many opponents of the tsar, whose secret police dispatched countless would-be revolutionaries to the frozen lands of Siberia.

Vladimir Kollontai worked as an engineer and, in January of 1896, took his young bride to visit the Krengholm textile factory in Narva, a city to the west of Saint Petersburg. He and a team of engineers planned to install a new ventilator system to improve the air quality for the workers. Alexandra Kollontai spoke to some of the younger laborers, who told her that they toiled for eighteen-hour days locked up in the foul air of the factory and enjoyed only a few hours off on Sunday. Airborne textile fibers compromised their lungs, and tuberculosis circulated viciously in the barracks. Many workers died after only three or four years of employment. Twelve thousand workers lived in cramped company lodgings, sleeping on flimsy bunk beds or scattered across the floor. Children spent their days alone and neglected in the squalor of the dormitories. "I was given permission to spend my days in the factory, and it made such a profound impression on me that it changed my whole life," Kollontai later told an American war correspondent for the *San Francisco Bulletin*. "I went away feeling I could not live unless I did something to help change the condition of the Russian workers. I knew no Socialists, but I began to read, and found my way to Socialism through books."[5]

Among the many books she devoured, she took particular interest in August Bebel's 1879 *Woman and Socialism* and Friedrich Engels's 1884 *The Origin of the Family, Private Property, and the State*. Written while he was imprisoned for supporting the Paris Commune, Bebel's influential book was translated into twenty languages and had fifty editions by the outbreak of World War I in 1914.[6] Through the work of Bebel and Engels, as well as other key socialist theorists, Kollontai began to understand how women's fates were intricately bound to the prevailing economic mode of production. Family relations, specifically the monogamous nuclear family, underpinned the ideological structures that were upholding private property. Mothers literally manufactured the next generation of workers and soldiers for the tsar and Russia's economic elites even as they labored for paltry wages in the putrid air of the textile mills. As mothers and workers, they were doubly exploited by the owners of the means of production. Although she agreed with Bebel and Engels that women needed to become economically independent of men through formal participation in the labor force, Kollontai knew that this would not be enough. As a wife and mother struggling against social expectations about the appropriate place of women, Kollontai intuited that socialism required more than just the collective ownership of the means of production. It necessitated an entirely new form of social relations in the home.

Following Bebel and Engels, she identified the monogamous nuclear family as the primary institution in society responsible for the intergenerational transfer of wealth and privilege from fathers to their legitimate (born to legally married parents) heirs. Women's bodies were as much a means of production as any textile mill or steam engine. Laws which rendered wives the property of their husbands for the purpose of producing these legitimate heirs turned women into commodities. In her 1909 pamphlet "The Social Basis of the Woman Question," Kollontai wrote: "In the family of today, the structure of which is confirmed by custom and law, woman is oppressed not only as a person but as a wife and mother, in most of the countries of the civilised world the civil code places women in a greater or lesser dependence on her husband and awards the husband not only the right to dispose of her property but also the right of moral and physical dominance over her."[7]

One of Kollontai's key insights was to unpack the relationship between traditional forms of patriarchy and the emergent political economy of capitalism in Russia in the late nineteenth century. For women to break free from millennia of male domination, they needed to help build a workers' state which fully socialized the reproductive labor that women performed in the home. Rather than merely outsourcing this labor to poorer women as private servants, governesses, cooks, and so forth, Kollontai imagined a fundamental shift in the basis of household relations that would allow for the collective and public provision of domestic work, freeing women to achieve economic independence from their fathers and husbands. She explains:

On the ruins of the former family we shall soon behold rising a new form which will involve altogether different relations between men and women, and which will be a *union of affection and comradeship, a union of two equal persons of the Communist Society, both of them free, both of them independent, both of them workers*. No more domestic "servitude" for women! No more inequality within the family. No more fear on the part of the woman to remain without support or aid with the little ones in her arms if her husband should desert her. The woman in the Communist city no longer depends on her husband but on her own work. It is not her husband but her robust arms which will support her.[8]

Upon her return from Narva, Kollontai began agitating among female textile workers in Saint Petersburg, distributing literature and raising money to support women's strikes against Russia's greedy industrialists. Although Saint Petersburg had a nascent feminist movement, Kollontai had no interest in expanding rights for already privileged women. "The feminists seek equality in the framework of the existing class society, in no way do they attack the basis of this society. They fight for prerogatives for themselves, without challenging the existing prerogatives and privileges."[9] As a Marxist, Kollontai asserted that working women needed to cooperate with working men to overthrow the tsarist regime. Only together could they build a new society in which workers and peasants could benefit from the collective ownership of land, factories, and machines.

Kollontai taught evening classes to workers and organized underground networks to help political prisoners and other socialist activists persecuted by the secret police. As she immersed herself in the revolutionary struggle, she grew

Young Alexandra Kollontai

distant from her husband whom she still loved, but whose political imagination only went as far as building better ventilators. Because tsarist Russia limited higher educational opportunities for women, Alexandra Kollontai decided to leave her husband and young son to pursue further studies in economics at the University of Zurich in 1898. Once there, she encountered many Russian and Western European students and activists inspired by the same Marxist ideals. At university, Kollontai buried herself in books once more, further radicalizing her views about the relationship between women, the family, and the economy. Although shy and introverted as a young woman, she soon honed her oratorical skills. As with Pavlichenko, Kollontai discovered her talent for public speaking.

When Kollontai returned to Russia in 1903, she dedicated herself to the work of the Social Democratic Labor Party to help agitate among women. Now estranged from her husband, she set up a household with her young son and her Bulgarian friend, Zoya Shadurskaya. Kollontai and Shadurskaya had first met in Bulgaria as children in 1878, and had developed a special bond that lasted throughout their lifetimes. Shadurskaya went to Saint Petersburg to live with her newlywed friend after the birth of Kollontai's son, Misha, followed Kollontai into exile in Western Europe between 1908 and 1917, lived with Alexandra and Misha in Moscow in the early years after the October Revolution, and frequently visited Kollontai while she served as a diplomat in Norway and Sweden. Shadurskaya never married and supported herself as a writer and a journalist, making it easy to pick up her life and relocate when necessary—the very embodiment of Kollontai's vision of "the new woman." Kollontai described Shadurskaya as "the dearest person in the world to me, apart from my son," and Zoya's friendship and loyalty would outlast any of Kollontai's marriages or love affairs. "Friendship is a more sociable emotion than sexual love," Kollontai later explained when discussing her decades-long relationship with Shadurskaya. "You can have many friends at a time, because there are different strings which vibrate in contact with different people."[10] Kollontai understood the inability of monogamous romantic love to fulfil every emotional need, and although she approved of polyamorous relationships, she would have argued that poly-amory also required developing friendship, comradeship, and kinship ties in addition to romantic ones.

During Kollontai's time working in the Russian under-ground (both before and after her participation in the failed 1905 revolution), she developed close friendships with many other revolutionaries and began to formulate ideas about "comradely love." "The stronger the ties of all members of the collective," Kollontai explained in 1921, "the less the need for the creation of strong marital relations."[11] Kollontai argued that, in societies in which people were isolated and drained by the daily grind of economic competition and the basic struggle to survive, they placed inordinate demands on their romantic relationships. Her observations resonate today. As Kollontai wrote in 1921:

> The ideal of the bourgeoisie was the married couple, where the partners complemented each other so completely that they had no need of contact with society. Communist morality demands, on the contrary, that the younger generation be educated in such a way that the personality of the individual is developed to the full, and the individual with his or her many interests has contact with a range of persons of both sexes. Communist morality encourages the development of many and varied bonds of love and friendship among people.[12]

In Kollontai's vision of the future socialist society, the expansion of social safety nets and the socialization of domes-tic labor would reduce the stresses of everyday life. Ordinary

Saint Kollontai and the Dragon of Jealousy by Paolo
Uccello (1475) and Elisheva Levy (2018)

people would have access to collective resources such as apartments, canteens, and laundries, which would meet at least their basic material needs. No one would have to marry for money, food, clothing, or shelter. "As regards sexual relations, communist morality demands first of all an end to all relations based on financial or other economic considerations," she explained.[13] Once disentangled from these economic considerations, romantic partners would be chosen solely on the basis of love, attraction, and mutual affection. And those romantic relationships would be embedded within an expansive network of friendships with colleagues and comrades who would all be available for different forms of intellectual companionship or emotional support. Kollontai tried to live her own life freed from the ideal of bourgeois romantic love. Although she had husbands and lovers, the core people in her life were her son, Zoya, and her comrades in the party. The revolutionary cause was Kollontai's true love, and she forged deep bonds with all those who fought for the same goals, bonds which nourished and sustained her.

In 1907, Kollontai attended the First International Conference of Socialist Women in Stuttgart, Germany, where she hardened her disagreements with those she considered bourgeois feminists. "The women's world is divided, just as is the world of men, into two camps; the interests and aspirations of one group of women bring it close to the bourgeois class, while the other group has close connections with the proletariat, and its claims for liberation encompass a full solution to the woman question," Kollontai wrote in 1909. "Thus although both camps follow the general slogan of the 'liberation of women,' their aims and interests are different."[14] Kollontai's struggle against wealthy women was equaled (if not surpassed) by her battle to get her male comrades to take women's issues seriously. Even basic educational agitation among women workers was viewed as tangential to the larger goals of the revolution, and some of Kollontai's own women comrades insisted that there should be no separate women's organization within the party because it might antagonize the men. Kollontai reflected on her efforts to organize Russian women in 1908:

> My Party comrades accused me and those women-comrades who shared my views of being "feminists" and of placing too much emphasis on matters of concern to women only ... I demanded from the Party that it espouse the cause of women's liberation. I did not always have an easy time of it. Much passive resistance, little understanding, and even less interest for this aim, over and over again, lay as an obstacle in the path.[15]

But Kollontai was tenacious. By emphasizing that a focus on women's issues would grow the strength of the worker's movement, she fought to convince her comrades that special agitation among working women was necessary to bring them into the wider proletarian struggle. Because women workers were generally less educated and less politically aware than their male comrades (many were illiterate), different tactics had to be deployed. And since their obligations as wives and mothers limited their available time for participation in illegal political meetings or educational circles, the socialists needed to find creative ways to reach women in the workplace. Kollontai also understood that women workers had different immediate demands than men and that activists would need to appeal to women's specific problems to bring them into the revolutionary fold, particularly around issues of maternity leave and childcare. Following the example of Clara Zetkin in Germany, Kollontai advocated for the creation of women's sections *within* the larger umbrella of the social democratic, socialist, or communist parties. "An independent grouping of proletarian women within the party has clear organizational advantages," Kollontai wrote in 1907. "Such an organization would make it possible to concentrate the attention of the party on the specific needs and requirements of women workers, and would also make it easier to rally around the party the generally less aware female members of the proletarian class."[16]

From her own experiences in Saint Petersburg, Kollontai knew that working men failed to understand the necessary role of the woman question within the larger socialist cause, particularly as the number of women workers grew in the textile industry. Russian capitalists preferred female labor because it was cheaper, more docile, and less prone to alcoholism. Many proletarian men initially resented the increasing presence of women in the factories and criticized their own wives when they attended meetings or classes rather than performing their domestic duties. But rather than abandoning men for their chauvinism, Kollontai insisted that women socialists must educate them:

In order to inculcate in their comrades the proper attitude to the question of equal rights for women workers in every sphere and draw them into the struggle to attain in practice equal civil rights for women, women have only one course—to unite their forces around the party. Women workers must set up a women's secretariat, a commission, a bureau within the party, not in order to wage a separate battle for political rights and defend their own interests by themselves but in order to exert pressure on the party *from within,* in order to compel their comrades to wage their struggle in the interests of the female proletariat as well.[17]

This insistence on working together with her male comrades within existing party structures would eventually make Kollontai the most powerful woman in the first Bolshevik government.

Kollontai's political work began to attract the attention of the authorities, and she dodged several warrants for her arrest. Forced to flee Russia, Kollontai became an itinerant activist between 1908 and 1917. Together with Zetkin, Kollontai attended the Second International Congress of Socialist Women in Copenhagen in August 1910, just before the Eighth Congress of the Second International. In Denmark, the socialist women of early-twentieth-century Europe created a template for the policy recommendations that would form the program Kollontai implemented in the new Soviet Union just seven years later. The fourth item on their agenda—"Social Protection and Provision for Motherhood and Infants"— demanded an eight-hour working day and a prohibition on the labor of children under fourteen years old. Pregnant women would have the right to stop work eight weeks before delivery and new mothers would enjoy a paid maternity leave of another eight weeks if the child lived. An additional five weeks would be granted to nursing mothers. All working women would enjoy these benefits, including agricultural laborers and domestic workers not just those in the factories. To fund these programs, states would establish dedicated maternity funds out of tax revenues. This public provision of support for women's caregiving duties would eventually become a hallmark of progressive societies around the world, including many postcolonial countries pursuing a socialist path to development in the Global South.[18]

But the outbreak of World War I created an irreparable rift in the European socialist community. The Social Democrats of almost all countries abandoned their commitments to internationalism and rushed headlong into the conflagration. Alexandra Kollontai, Clara Zetkin, Rosa Luxemburg, and other women activists raged against the betrayal of the German Social Democratic Party and the other Menshevik-style parties in Europe. All of these parties had once condemned war as a tool of bourgeois imperialism and called for the unity of the working classes of all nations. But when World War I started, they decided in favor of the "defense of the fatherland," especially the Germans who voted unanimously to extend war credits to the kaiser. How could men who had experienced the miserable conditions of proletarian life suddenly rush to defend the very bourgeois classes that exploited them?

Vladimir Lenin, with whom Kollontai had worked in Paris, took an extreme position on the war. Whereas Kollontai initially embraced pacifism (in the tradition of Leo Tolstoy), Lenin believed that the soldiers of all countries should seize the opportunity to use their guns and weapons to start civil wars against their respective governments. In the first year of the conflict, nationalist sentiments won out and the Bolshevik position was rejected. But, as the war dragged on, the appeal of the Bolsheviks grew. Lenin's principled stance against an imperialist war finally drew Kollontai away from the Mensheviks, demonstrating her receptivity to new perspectives and a willingness to change her political orientation in response to unforeseen historical events. By 1915 she had become a regular correspondent and collaborator with Lenin, his wife, Nadezhda Krupskaya, and their comrade Inessa Armand.

Between 1911 and 1916, Kollontai also began a prolonged, on-and-off affair with the Bolshevik Alexander Shlyapnikov, a Russian metal worker and trade union leader also exiled in Western Europe (who would later become the People's Commissar of Labor). They met in Paris in late 1911 when Kollontai was thirty-nine and Shlyapnikov was twenty-six. According to Kollontai's diaries, there was a strong "spark" between them despite their differences in age and social class.[19] In some of Lenin's correspondence from this era, he referred to Kollontai as Shlyapnikov's "wife," although the two were never married.[20] In addition to their romance, Kollontai and Shlyapnikov developed a close political relationship, smuggling literature into Russia through Scandinavia on a "Northern Railroad" of sympathetic couriers. Long before electronic communications were possible, the illegal passing of newspapers, pamphlets, and messages across borders required complicated logistics and absorbed the time and energy of many exiles.[21] Kollontai and Shlyapnikov's working relationship and friendship long outlasted their affair.

In late 1915, American socialists invited Kollontai to do a paid four-month tour around the United States, speaking on socialism, women's rights, and pacifism. She visited eighty-one cities and delivered 123 lectures in four languages, impressing American socialist audiences from coast to coast with her oratorical abilities.[22] She briefly spent time in New York and later lived for some months in Paterson, New Jersey, where her son had enrolled in an engineering course. Kollontai's travels in the United States revealed to her the deep class fissures lurking behind the lofty narratives of the American dream (as Pavlichenko had discovered during her tour twenty-seven years later). "During those four and a half months," Kollontai wrote after her lecture tour, "I had seen politicians insistently preaching in favour of militarism and the bitter struggle waged by labour against unrestrained American capital, the power wielded by the American police and the omnipotence of the trust kings, the corruption of American courts, the servility of the American capitalist press."[23] In a short essay reflecting on the Statue of Liberty, the symbol that had "once caused the hearts of our European fathers and grandfathers to beat with triumphant happiness and exultation," Kollontai came to understand that the United States no longer held out the promise of freedom to the poor and downtrodden.

As World War I dragged on, Russians grew increasingly angry at the prolonged economic upheavals and human costs of the conflict. In February 1917, after centuries of autocracy, a series of spontaneous strikes, women's demonstrations, mutinies, and violent clashes forced the abdication of the Russian tsar. Suddenly, control of the vast empire fell to a bourgeois provisional government. Kollontai rushed back to Saint Petersburg (now Petrograd), where she led the city's laundresses in the first strike under the new government of Alexander Kerensky, who had her arrested and imprisoned for two months. She was eventually released on bail and put under house arrest.[24] Since the Provisional Government refused to withdraw from the disastrous World War I, Kollontai rallied for the Bolsheviks, becoming an invaluable ally of Lenin and ultimately voting in favor of armed insurrection to seize power. After the October revolution, Lenin named Kollontai the Commissar for Social Welfare on October 28, 1917.

The immediate aftermath of the revolution saw Kollontai at the very center of power. She set about realizing her long-standing ambition for women's emancipation, the abolition of the sexual double standard, and the creation of a new socialist morality that liberated women from the social mores that bound them in domestic servitude within the family. In December 1917, with the help of a cadre of progressive Soviet lawyers, Kollontai orchestrated the passage of two decrees replacing church marriage with civil marriage and liberalizing divorce. When the American journalist Louise Bryant met her in 1918, she found herself in awe of Kollontai's work ethic: "She works untiringly and, through persistence born of flaming intensity, she accomplishes a tremendous amount."[25]

In October 1918, the highest legislative body of the Soviet Union incorporated these decrees into a new Family Law: the Code of Laws concerning the Civil Registration of Deaths, Births and Marriages.[26] The Code ruptured many centuries of patriarchal and ecclesiastical authority, overturning all laws that rendered women the property of their fathers and husbands and abolishing the church's control over marriage and divorce. Women earned juridical equality with men, married women retained complete control over their own wages, and the new Code ensured that all children received parental support and orphans guaranteed state guardianship.

Kollontai also proposed a vast network of communally run state laundries, cafeterias, and children's centers. Once women had been liberated from the duties of the home, Kollontai hoped that they would enter the public sphere on equal terms with men, pursuing their education and careers as they desired. As women developed their skills and talents, they would gain agency and control of their own lives, earning their own income in professions now open to members of both sexes. Financially independent women would be able to choose their romantic partners out of love and mutual affection rather than relying on the crass economic calculation that typified bourgeois marriages.

The new Code embodied the essence of Kollontai's grand plan for women's equality and the eventual obsolescence of the bourgeois monogamous family. After its passage, divorce rates skyrocketed as Russian women were finally free to leave abusive or alcoholic husbands and Russian men abandoned women they had been forced to marry after getting them pregnant. Kollontai imagined that this liberalization would usher in an era of new relationships based on her concept of "comradely love." For his part, Lenin cared little for Kollontai's intimate politics, but he did agree that women's housework was unproductive drudgery. Russia had lost many men in World War I, and Lenin needed Kollontai to mobilize Russia's women to defend the new state no matter the cost. The revolution's very survival depended on women's participation in the formal labor force and, for at least the first decade, the Bolsheviks were willing to challenge the very foundations of traditional family life if it created more workers to prop up the faltering economy.

Kollontai held her ministerial position until March 28, 1918, when she resigned in protest against the appalling terms of the treaty of Brest-Litovsk (which got Russia out of World War I but with huge territorial concessions to the Germans).[27] Still committed to her work for women, Kollontai won herself a key victory when the Eighth Congress of the Communist Party passed her resolution demanding an intensification of the party's work among women in 1919. The Congress committed itself to further growing the number of socialized laundries, cafeterias, and children's homes.[28] That same year, Kollontai, together with Inessa Armand, helped to create the *Zhenotdel*, a special women's section established within the Central Committee of the Communist Party.[29] In 1920, the Soviet Union also became the first country in the world to legalize abortion on demand during the first twelve weeks of pregnancy.[30]

The years between 1919 and 1923 would be years of constant chaos and tumult as Russia lurched from revolution to civil war to famine to a New Economic Policy, which was a partial reversion to the capitalism that Kollontai abhorred. In early 1918, she had also agreed to marry her new lover, a Ukrainian peasant who had become a Kronstadt sailor and ultimately the leader of the Baltic Fleet. Pavel Dybenko was sixteen years her junior, and the difference in their ages and social positions scandalized even the most progressive Bolsheviks. Lenin worried that Kollontai's unseemly love affairs distracted from the serious work of building a new government. To dispel the vicious gossip, Dybenko wanted to formalize their relationship under the new system of civil marriages. At the time, Zoya Shadurskaya feared that Dybenko would interfere with Kollontai's revolutionary aspirations for women. "Will you really put down our flag of freedom for his sake?" Zoya told her childhood friend. "You, who all your life have been fighting against the slavery that married life brings and that always comes into collision with our work and achievements?"[31] Zoya's warning proved prescient: Kollontai and Dybenko's marriage did not last long, especially after Kollontai suffered a serious heart attack in 1919. In 1920, Dybenko found himself a younger woman who had more time to cater to her husband's needs.

In 1920, Kollontai, Shadurskaya, and Kollontai's son, Misha, were living together with other Bolsheviks at the Hotel

Pavel Dybenko and Alexandra Kollontai in 1920

National in Moscow. It was here that the American anarchist Emma Goldman first met the woman whom Karl Radek would call a "Valkyrie" on the floor of the meetings of the Third Communist International in 1921[32]: "Mme. Kollontay looked remarkably young and radiant, considering her fifty years and the severe operation she had recently undergone," Goldman wrote of her first impression of Kollontai. "A tall and stately woman, every inch the *grande dame* rather than the fiery revolutionist. Her attire and suite of two rooms bespoke good taste, the roses on her desk rather startling in the Russian greyness."[33] Yet the trials of the civil war and the constant demands of governance weighed heavily on Kollontai during this time, especially when she assumed the leadership of the Zhenotdel after the sudden death of Inessa Armand in September 1920.

During Goldman's time in the USSR, various leftist factions began turning on each other, particularly with regard to the independence of the trade unions. Vladimir Lenin and Leon Trotsky demanded centralized control of the state and economy, which minimized the power and influence of the workers' councils who had supported them. Kollontai aligned herself with her old lover and friend Shlyapnikov in defending the rights of the workers to self-management, a movement variously called the Workers' Opposition, the Labor Opposition, or the Left Opposition. Although Kollontai understood the need for a centralized state, she sympathized with the workers' demands for autonomy and self-governance. Emma Goldman abhorred the bureaucracy she saw forming in the new Soviet government. In many ways, Kollontai agreed with her American anarchist comrade that workers should maintain control over their enterprises. At a Party Congress in late 1920, there were four competing views on the fate of the trade unions. Emma Goldman, who attended the proceedings, agreed with Shlyapnikov and Kollontai, and bristled at their treatment:

At the Congress, Lenin denounced the Labour Opposition as "anarcho-syndicalist, middle-class ideology" and advocated its entire suppression. Shlyapnikov, one of the most influential leaders of the Opposition, was referred to by Lenin as a "peeved Commissar" and was subsequently silenced by being made a member of the Central Committee of the Communist Party. Madame Kollontay was told to hold her tongue or get out of the Party; her pamphlet setting forth the views of the Opposition was suppressed.[34]

The pamphlet Goldman mentions was Kollontai's thoughtful enumeration of the disagreements that she and the rest of the Workers' Opposition had with the Soviet government's current policies. She meant it as constructive criticism from within the party ranks by one of its most loyal supporters. But Kollontai's open opposition to Lenin and Trotsky severely damaged her political future in Moscow. The men belittled her support for the Workers' Opposition as evidence that she had reignited her relationship with Shlyapnikov following her break with Dybenko (she had not). Even worse for Kollontai was the betrayal of Shlyapnikov. He distanced himself from her after the Congress and assured Lenin and Trotsky that Kollontai's pamphlet represented her views alone. Later, Kollontai continued to criticize Lenin for his New Economic Policy, which she considered a political reversal that allowed for the limited reintroduction of markets and drastically worsened the living conditions of working women.[35] Faced with slander and ridicule by her own comrades—and following her bitter divorce from Dybenko (who had illegally requisitioned new clothes for his young lover under Kollontai's name)—she asked Stalin (who was in charge of political assignments) to find her a position outside of Moscow so she could escape the political infighting.

Writing in 1923, Louise Bryant reflected on Kollontai's persistent challenges to her Bolshevik comrades:

Madame Kollontai's political judgment, even from the stand-
point of an orthodox Communist, is often very bad. She has
unlimited courage and on several occasions has openly opposed
Lenin. As for Lenin, he has crushed her with his usual unruffled
frankness. Yet in spite of her fiery enthusiasm she understands
"party discipline" and takes defeat like a good soldier. If she
had left the revolution four months after it began she could
have rested forever on her laurels. She seized those rosy first
moments of elation, just after the masses had captured the
state, to incorporate into the Constitution laws for women
which are far-reaching and unprecedented. And the Soviets are
very proud of these laws which already have around them the
halo of all things connected with the Constitution.[36]

But many of these far-reaching and unprecedented laws
would not survive Stalin's reign. If Kollontai's support for the
Workers' Opposition proved fruitless, so too did many of her
attempts to improve the lives of Soviet women. The historians
Elizabeth Wood and Wendy Goldman have well documented
how Kollontai's attempts to remake Russian society in the
1920s largely ended in failure.[37] Kollontai's male comrades
never fully supported her; they continued to harbor suspicions
that her insistence on women's issues would split the solidarity of the working class. Many of the Bolshevik leaders also
disapproved of Kollontai's theories promoting a new communist sexual morality. They ridiculed her after the publication
of her scandalous short story "The Loves of Three Generations" and her similarly controversial essay, "Make Way for
Winged Eros: A Letter to Working Youth."

Both published in 1923, these writings represent perhaps
the two most provocative Russian texts about sexuality of the
early twentieth century. In "The Loves of Three Generations,"
Kollontai investigates changing sexual moralities through
a tale of three women: grandmother, daughter, and granddaughter. The daughter comes to speak with a Kollontai-like

character to inquire whether or not she is being a bourgeois prude for disapproving of a casual sexual relationship between her daughter and her second husband (that is, between the granddaughter and the granddaughter's stepfather). Kollontai explores the emotion of jealousy, and while she accepts that it is natural, she argues that it can be overcome if people stop viewing their lovers as property. She also downplays the significance of sexual relations in women's lives, especially when compared to the importance of revolutionary work on behalf of the collective.

In "Make Way for Winged Eros," Kollontai lays out a political economy of love whereby both men and women are free to have multiple partners (sexual, emotional, intellectual, or otherwise) in a society with stronger collective bonds. As in "The Loves of Three Generations," the essay's central argument is that the harshness and precarity of capitalist life make people cling to each other in unhealthy ways. Rather than acting as kindred souls working together toward common goals, lovers often demand exclusive rights to each other's sexual and emotional attentions. But Kollontai's arguments were misunderstood as a call for callous promiscuity, and the Soviet press attacked her. Her aristocratic background, her multiple lovers, and her penchant for younger, working-class men—combined with her open political support for the Workers' Opposition and criticism of the New Economic Policy—eroded her domestic political credibility. After her personal appeal to Stalin, Kollontai left for Norway as a member of the Soviet legation. Within a year, she had become the first Russian woman ambassador and only the third woman ambassador in the world, beginning a diplomatic career that would keep her out of the Soviet Union until the end of World War II.

Kollontai's theories about love and sex were decades ahead of their time. As she argued for a political economy of love, the fledging state of the Soviet Union was reeling from years of conflict. The chaos of World War I and the civil war combined with a severe drought to precipitate a horrendous famine. The Bolsheviks lacked the resources to socialize all domestic work; public laundries, canteens, and childcare facilities cost too much for the struggling Soviet economy. And, in some cases, the very laws meant to liberate Russian women allowed men to become more cavalier in their paternal responsibilities, making women's lives harder. By 1926, many women, especially in the rural areas, were clamoring for a return to the old ways. Their paltry wages were not enough to support children on their own, liberalized divorce laws meant that men abandoned women at the first sign of a pregnancy, and alimony provisions proved almost impossible to enforce. In the absence of reliable forms of birth control, free love produced hundreds of thousands of unplanned and often unwanted pregnancies. Because the state lacked the resources to care for them, homeless children swarmed the major cities. The 1920 liberalization of abortion allowed women to control their fertility, but this then precipitated a massive and (for the government) undesirable plunge in the birth rate. Given the choice, many women preferred to forgo motherhood, but the world's first workers' state needed more workers.

Kollontai's inspired attempt to liberate women from centuries of patriarchal control also unleashed the worst in Soviet men. No longer the private property of their fathers and husbands, women faced an avalanche of sexual violence. Fyodor Gladkov's 1925 novel *Cement* deals explicitly with sexual violence in the immediate aftermath of the revolution, as does the 1926 "discussion play" by Sergei Tetryakov, *I Want a Baby*. Tetryakov's honest depictions of gang rape and sexual harassment—an explicit recognition of the challenges Soviet women faced in trying to take advantage of their new rights and privileges—resulted in his play being censored and ultimately banned.[38] More importantly, many Russian men refused to treat women as their equals and pined for the days of women's previous subservience. Gladkov explored this theme in *Cement* when Gleb, a Red Army soldier, returns home to find that his wife, Dasha, has become a newly liberated Soviet woman and moved their daughter into a collective children's home. In a key chapter called "The Cold Hearth," Gleb refuses to accept Dasha's independence and tries to rape her. She defends herself and declares that she is "not just a woman" but a "real person" who has fought for and earned the right to make decisions about her own life. The novel ends with Dasha leaving Gleb without so much as a backward glance.[39]

The 1927 Soviet silent film *Bed and Sofa* also depicts the tenacity of Russian patriarchy in the face of revolutionary change.[40] In this film, a married woman finds herself in a ménage à trois with her husband and his old Red Army comrade. Instead of being liberated by free love, the woman finds herself burdened with more domestic responsibilities to service the demands of two men instead of one. When the woman goes to get an abortion for an unplanned pregnancy, she decides to keep the baby and dumps the men. The final scene of the film finds her alone on a train, liberated from her marriage, and setting off to make a new future for herself and her child. But not all Soviet women enjoyed such happy endings; alcoholism and domestic violence plagued early Soviet family life.

In the short term, Kollontai's vision for a "new woman" choked on the impoverished realities of the weak Soviet economy and the stubborn resilience of traditional patriarchal norms. Despite these setbacks, Kollontai boldly published her *Autobiography of a Sexually Emancipated Communist Woman* in 1926. In the short and heavily censored book, she reflected on her life to date and assured her readers: "No matter what further tasks I shall be carrying out, it is perfectly clear to me that the complete liberation of the working woman and the creation of the foundation of a new sexual morality will always remain the highest aim of my activity, and of my life."[41] The provisions of the original 1918 Family Code were slowly reversed. Stalin did away with the most progressive aspects of the earlier laws in 1936, when a revised Family Code banned abortion and discouraged divorce, reintroducing the traditional patriarchal family as a basic unit of Soviet life.

Alexandra Kollontai spent most of her remaining years serving in diplomatic posts in Norway, Mexico, and Sweden. The Spaniard Isabel de Palencia worked closely with Kollontai in Stockholm on the eve of World War II and marveled at Kollontai's ability to maneuver in a sometimes hostile diplomatic milieu. In her own autobiography, Palencia described Kollontai as a close friend and as

> a woman of extraordinary intelligence, keen vision, and unconquerable will, together with a warm heart. It is no wonder that in the face of all opposition she should have managed to make a place for herself even in such antagonistic circles … Alexandra Kollontay is above all things an idealist. Her political creed may not be to everyone's taste, but one is forced to respect her for her absolute loyalty to what she judges best for the world's happiness.[42]

Perhaps because of her valuable skills as a diplomat, Kollontai survived Stalin's purges of the Old Bolsheviks, which claimed the lives of many of her personal friends, including Shlyapnikov in 1937 and Dybenko in 1938. Kollontai herself was recalled to Moscow in 1937 and feared the worst, but Stalin allowed her return to Stockholm. Zoya Shadurskaya also died in Leningrad in 1939, and Kollontai worried for the safety of her son and his family. Palencia painted a poignant portrait of an aging Kollontai helpless to intervene in Stalin's terror. Palencia writes: "During those anxious days, my heart ached for Alexandra … I was anxious about her because I knew she must feel that death penalties are so irretrievable that one must hesitate in their application. And there was, for her, the additional agony from the fact that those men had been her friends and comrades."[43] One day, at the height of the purges, Kollontai asked Palencia to drive with her out to the forests surrounding Stockholm and to take a walk far from where the spies and informants might hear their conversation. Palencia recalls:

> That day I thought she looked ill, not worried. Her features were drawn and pale but her eyes lighted up as she turned to me while the car sped swiftly down the road that led to a forest nearby, one of her favorite haunts. I held out my hand and she clasped it in hers. But we did not exchange a single word until we were facing the narrow walks under the giant firs hung with icicles, their whiteness melting into soft bluish tones under the facing light. Alexandra looked up at them, breathed deeply, and then turned to me and said, "There was a time when all our men seemed as straight and firm and pure as these." And her eyes glistening with unshed tears, she opened her heart to me. Some of the men who had been tried had been her dear comrades. One she mentioned with quivering lips was her doctor ... "Life confronts us with many things that are difficult to understand," she said after a long pause.[44]

Although Kollontai once challenged Lenin, Trotsky, and the other Old Bolsheviks on matters of principle, she accommodated herself to Stalin's rule, even though he had undone most of her work for women and undermined the socialization of domestic labor. Kollontai cooperated with him throughout the 1930s and 1940s, and even after her return to the Soviet Union following World War II. She often praised the USSR and its leaders for their heroic defeat of fascism and for making the Soviet woman "a full and equal citizen of her country."[45] Perhaps it was out of fear for the safety of her son and grandson; Stalin had killed many of her comrades and she knew he could be ruthless. Or maybe it was sheer pragmatism; Kollontai hated Hitler and other fascists and perhaps believed that Stalin was Europe's only chance of repelling Nazi aggression. It is also possible that she was just exhausted from a long life of political struggle. Standing up for her beliefs had achieved little in the 1920s. In 1936, Kollontai confided in her former first secretary, the French communist Marcel Body, that the bloodshed of the purges was unavoidable given the circumstances. Kollontai told Body "that Russia could not pass in a few years from absolutism to freedom" and that "historically, Russia, with its innumerable masses without culture, without discipline, is not ripe for democracy."[46]

Despite her quasi exile from the center of Soviet politics, Kollontai enjoyed a long and celebrated diplomatic career and was twice nominated for the Nobel Peace Prize (in 1946 and 1947) for her negotiation of the Soviet–Finnish peace after the Winter War.[47] On March 28, 2017, the eve of what would have been her 145th birthday, the Russian foreign minister Sergei Lavrov officially dedicated a new commemorative plaque in her honor:

Alexandra Kollontai and her son, Misha

74

Alexandra Kollontai was a legend, a remarkable public figure and politician, the first woman ambassador to represent our country abroad ... She dedicated almost 35 years of her life to the Foreign Ministry ... As ambassador to Sweden, Alexandra Kollontai made a major contribution to ensuring that our relations with Sweden and other Scandinavian countries remained on a solid footing, as well as to prevent them from being influenced by Hitler's Germany. One of the real achievements of this remarkable woman was that she took part in negotiations that led to Finland's withdrawal from the war in 1944, which helped free up troops and send them to other fronts, saving lives of many Soviet soldiers.[48]

My favorite story about Kollontai from the 1940s is one of a random act of kindness she herself probably forgot soon after it happened.[49] Back in 2010, the communications office of Bowdoin College asked me to write a short piece about a feminist figure I admired for International Women's Day. When my reflection went live, I received an email from a senior colleague in the German Department: "If it weren't for Madam Kollontai, I would never have been born!"

Intrigued, I asked my colleague Steven Cerf for more details. In 1940, after the Nazis had overrun Norway, Professor Cerf's father, Hans Cerf, found himself in the Soviet embassy in Stockholm. Having escaped from a concentration camp, Hans and his wife (my colleague's parents) needed Soviet transit visas to get out of Europe before what they feared was the imminent invasion of Sweden. After an initial inquiry, the Soviet clerk told Hans that visas required six weeks of background investigations. In that instant, Hans Cerf recounted: "The door opened and a beautiful bosomy lady—all in black— stormed in, in a hurry. Momentarily I realized that this must be Madame Kollontai, the Russian ambassador to Sweden. 'Now, Hans, I said to myself, where is your Russian?'... I stepped before the lady: 'Listen comrade Kollontai, I am a comrade too, and I have to get out NOW!'"[50]

Apparently, Kollontai looked him up and down and decided she liked him. She turned to her clerk and ordered him to grant the visa. Hans hastily explained that he also needed one for his wife. "Give him two!" Kollontai commanded and disappeared. As the rare woman in a position of power, Kollontai used her authority to ensure that Hans and Kate Cerf escaped, and I had the pleasure of meeting their son all of those years later in Maine. "Madam Kollontai is a hero in our family!" Professor Cerf wrote to me back in 2010.

After 1945, Kollontai suffered from increasingly ill health. Two strokes left her partially paralyzed, and she struggled against all of the common indignities of advanced age. She spent her waning days consulting for the Soviet Ministry of Foreign Affairs and organizing her personal papers, hoping that her life story would be an inspiration to those who came after her.

In the late summer of 1946, Kollontai sent a letter to her old friend Isabel de Palencia, detailing her life back home in the Soviet Union: "The winter was very exciting and interesting for me, there is so much enthusiasm and life in Russia and everyone is so very kind to me. I am still working on my memoirs and some parts are already published here in Russia. I feel better. And now I am going for a rest to a beautiful place near Moscow. So in the autumn I will be able to take up my work and duties."[51] After one last vacation to restore her strength, and still hoping to build a better future for Soviet women, Alexandra Kollontai died at the age of seventy-nine, less than a month before her eightieth birthday in 1952. "One must write not only for oneself," she explained in her memoirs. "But for others. For those far away, unknown women who will live then. Let them see that we were not heroines or heroes after all. But we believed passionately and ardently. We believed in our goals and we pursued them. Sometimes we were strong and sometimes we were very weak."[52]

3

The Radical Pedagogue

Nadezhda Krupskaya (1869–1939)

Although Alexandra Kollontai is arguably the best remembered of the three revolutionary-era Red Valkyries, she would have been the first to recognize the important contributions of the two comrades who most fervently shared her passion for socialist women's emancipation: Inessa Armand and Nadezhda Krupskaya. Although Krupskaya was more conservative in her sexual life and often opposed Kollontai's more radical propositions about "winged eros," Kollontai described Krupskaya at her funeral in 1939 as "an extraordinary, outstanding personality, the most significant and splendid image of the Russian women in our great revolution. She was Lenin's staunch and indefatigable associate, friend and wife."[1]

After surviving three grueling years of Stalinist purges which claimed the lives of many of her closest comrades between 1937 and 1939, Krupskaya's heart gave out a day after her seventieth birthday. The *Chicago Daily Tribune* suggested that

Portrait of Nadezhda Krupskaya

"Krupskaya was probably glad to die."[2] The *New York Times* acknowledged that "her lot was not always an easy one," informing American readers: "After the seizure of power by the Bolsheviks, Mme. Krupskaya's greatest contribution to the Soviet regime was her work in educational and cultural fields … Throughout the succeeding years of the new regime Mme. Krupskaya pioneered for women's equality with men … Her slogan was, 'Down with domestic drudgery and illiteracy.'"[3] Leon Trotsky also paid tribute to Krupskaya from his exile in Mexico: "With profound sorrow we bid farewell to the loyal companion of Lenin, to an irreproachable revolutionist and one of the most tragic figures in revolutionary history."[4]

Despite the many indignities she endured after 1924, Krupskaya was the untiring workhorse of the revolution, utterly devoted to the cause of building the workers' state in the face of immense hardships: a paragon of engagement and tenacity. So monomaniacal was Krupskaya in her work that one of her biographers opined: "If the heavenly city of Communism could have been entered by dint of Krupskaya's labors, Russia would have become the world's first perfect society years ago."[5]

On February 14, 1869, Nadezhda Konstantinovna Krupskaya was born in the Saint Petersburg of Imperial Russia. After the abolition of feudalism in 1861, the Russian tsar understood that modern industrial economies required more educated working classes. Throughout the 1860s, the Russian state established hundreds of new adult literacy schools, and enacted laws for the expansion of education among all children in 1864.[6] Krupskaya's parents were impoverished nobles with a penchant for liberal thinking; her father nurtured anti-tsarist tendencies and her mother was uncommonly emancipated and educated for a woman of that time.[7] Although devoutly religious in her youth, Krupskaya was raised to be independent and self-sufficient in the turbulent atmosphere produced by the advent of Russian capitalism. For those growing up in an age where the old hierarchies were being radically challenged, progressive education and Marxist pedagogy provided key tools of social reform.

Intelligent and hardworking, Krupskaya achieved the highest level of education available to her in Russia at the time. She was a diligent student with a voracious appetite for reading, and developed a rare critical sensibility about the quality and purpose of the education she received. She enjoyed her experiences in secondary school, but her subsequent two months at the special Saint Petersburg *Bestuzhev* courses (special courses designed for daughters of the nobility who wanted access to higher educational opportunities and the only university-level classes available to her) were "too removed from real life," in her opinion.[8] But she had qualified to become a domestic tutor, and it was in teaching that Krupskaya discovered her true passion. Between 1891 and 1896, Krupskaya led adult courses at a special school for factory workers. She had been a fervent Tolstoyan in her youth and had sent letters to Tolstoy, who inspired her to spend some summer months trying to work with peasants and provide rudimentary lessons. Although there was a long tradition of the educated urban nobility trying to teach peasants, it seems her pedagogical efforts among them bore little fruit.

But factory workers flocked to her lessons. Despite problems of absenteeism and drunkenness, members of the urban proletariat craved educational opportunities, and Krupskaya felt immense personal satisfaction in her vocation. Spending every Sunday and two nights a week with the earnest men who came to learn after a grueling day's work opened her eyes to the harsh realities of proletarian life in 1890s Russia. In Krupskaya's vision of socialist pedagogy, influenced by Leo Tolstoy's own pedagogical experiments at Yasnaya Polyana beginning in 1859, the goal of education was to teach children and workers to think independently while also understanding the value of organized collective action.[9] Krupskaya, following Tolstoy, believed that an autocratic teacher standing at the front of a classroom full of docile and obedient children could not produce the type of citizens necessary for a self-managing socialist state. Where Tolstoy opposed compulsory education organized by the state, Krupskaya believed that only a workers' state could truly create classroom environments where pupils fully participated in their own learning. Sometimes this just meant sitting in a circle, but mostly it meant shaping education into a tool that working people could use to improve their lives. In a letter to Maxim Gorky, she explained that "the construction of socialism does not mean only the building of huge factories and grain mills: such things are necessary, but not in themselves sufficient for the construction of socialism. People must grow in mind and heart."[10]

Krupskaya was the first Russian socialist to dedicate a whole pamphlet to the situation of women. Written in 1899 under the pen name Sablina, "The Woman Worker" drew a disturbing portrait of the fate of women under Russian capitalism and in the traditional peasant family. Krupskaya specifically called upon Russian women to take up the struggle against autocracy, and painted an evocative picture of the better world that was possible if they joined the working-class movement:

> When production is managed by society everyone will have to work but labor will not be as arduous as it is today as everything will be done to lighten the unpleasant aspects of working and it will not be in stuffy, stinking and infected factories but in well lit, spacious, dry and well ventilated buildings. Labour will not be as lengthy as it is nowadays because all will work and, unlike today, one will not see some workers, including children and pregnant women, straining over their workload

while others are forced to be idle, jobless and looking hope-
lessly for work ... Society will take on itself the care for the
weak, the sick and the old ... People will not be afraid if they
fall ill that the family will be left destitute, as society as a whole
will be responsible for bringing up the children, caring for
them and making them strong healthy and intelligent, useful
and knowledgeable people, turned out as good citizens. Those
who want such a state of affairs and who fight to achieve it are
called socialists.[11]

Like Kollontai, Krupskaya held that socialist women
should work within extant party structures because she feared
division in the working class. But she also understood the
underlying chauvinism of Russian men and, like Kollontai,
walked a fine line between advocating for women's interests
while trying not to alienate her male comrades. "Stopping
women joining the struggle is the same as leaving half of the
workers' army unorganized," she wrote in 1899, detailing
how easily employers could use women as strike breakers
if men refused to bring them into the revolutionary struggle.[12] More importantly, Krupskaya admitted that proletarian
women generally had less interest in politics than men, were
prone to superstition, and were more likely to be burdened
with too many other cares. In fact, in 1899, the vast majority
of Russian women were illiterate. Knowing her audience,
Krupskaya used the simplest language possible to convince
women that they would only develop themselves politically
through active and repeated participation in strikes and
demonstrations. Among her ideas about socialist pedagogy,
Krupskaya believed that lived experience provided an essential pathway to education and that women could acquire
confidence and become radicalized only through joint action:

When there are confrontations with management she sees that
her comrades are always ready to back her up and she is to
support them. The same conflicts shows [sic.] her that while

she is weak when alone she ceases to be weak when she acts together with her comrades ... Collisions with the police and all kinds of authority, exiling and persecution of workers, the ban on discussing their affairs, the formation of unions make it clear that the government is on the side of the exalted and the rich. They teach her the necessity of political struggle and the necessity of winning for workers the right to take part in drawing up laws and in the way the country is run.[13]

Throughout her life, Krupskaya forged and strengthened her own confidence through engagement and confrontation. Together with Kollontai and Inessa Armand, she forced the development of the socialist women's movement, although she worked behind the scenes. In many ways, Krupskaya's life embodied her philosophy about collaborating with men for the greater cause, and while Lenin certainly gave her important responsibilities, he also relied on her to organize the couple's domestic affairs. Although Krupskaya kept her maiden name (unlike Kollontai, Pavlichenko, and Inessa Armand), she took pride in dealing with all of the quotidian necessities of human existence and in caring for her temperamental and demanding husband.

It was in 1894, while working in Saint Petersburg, that Krupskaya first met a certain young Marxist intellectual named Vladimir Ilyich Ulyanov, who later took the name Lenin.[14] Having dropped out of the boring *Bestuzhev* courses, she attended several informal circles where different groups gathered to discuss literary and political works. She recalled: "I lived on Staro-Nevsky Street at the time, in a building with a through courtyard, and Vladimir Ilyich used to drop in on Sundays after his circle work, when we would start endless conversations. I was in love with my school work and could talk about it for hours if you did not stop me."[15]

Krupskaya's dedication to her "school work" emerged from the solid foundation of her politics. In the memoir she wrote about her husband, *My Reminiscences of Lenin*, she revealed that she had embraced Marxism before she met him, believing that the autocracy could not be overthrown without the support of the urban proletariat. "It was a matter not of heroic deeds, but of establishing close contact with the masses, getting closer to them, learning to be the vehicle of their finest aspirations, learning how to win their confidence and rally them behind us."[16] Krupskaya regaled the young Lenin with stories about the aspirations and abilities of her proletarian students, and he took a deep interest in her knowledge of the working conditions in Saint Petersburg. Krupskaya admitted that Lenin was an "intellectual," which meant he hailed from the middle class and had no direct experience of proletarian life, but, unlike the other intellectuals she had met in radical circles, Lenin believed in applying theory to the real world. This impressed her.

Young and defiant Nadezhda Krupskaya

Little is known about their initial romance because Lenin and Krupskaya remained silent on the issue throughout their lives. But we do know that both young radicals took inspiration from a fictional character named Rakhmetov. Only a minor figure in Nikolai Chernyshevsky's 1863 novel *What Is to Be Done?*, Rakhmetov came to represent, for many nihilists and Marxists in late-nineteenth-century Russia, the ideal lifestyle necessary for a committed revolutionary. A celibate teetotaler, Rakhmetov hones his physical strength through daily exercise and regular participation in hard physical labor among the workers and peasants. When he is not developing his muscles, he spends hours reading books to develop his mind. He denies himself even the simplest luxuries, including a regular bed—he sleeps instead on a wooden plank. When he saves a young woman's life and she falls in love with him, Rakhmetov rejects her affections by explaining that his work for the freedom of the Russian people takes precedence over romantic love.

Rakhmetov's devotion to the cause and his strict asceticism formed the characters of both Lenin and Krupskaya. Chernyshevsky's novel was Lenin's favorite book, and he borrowed the title from it for his 1902 pamphlet. Photos of Krupskaya and descriptions of her from the records of the secret police reveal that she kept her appearance austere and simple. Where Kollontai wore furs, body-skimming dresses, and eyeliner and let her fashionably bobbed hair flow freely, Krupskaya pulled her hair straight back from her face and wore plain, conservative clothes. While these style choices might have partially derived from her earlier years as a Tolstoyan (Tolstoy also promoted asceticism), Rakhmetov's fictional example reaffirmed the appropriate comportment of a serious political radical who had better things to do than worry about romantic entanglements.

The events leading up to Krupskaya's marriage to Lenin suggest that it served at least partially as a convenient cover for their political activities. During the years they attended or taught in various political circles, the police surveilled them. Lenin was arrested in December of 1895, but so minimal was the connection between him and Krupskaya that the police ignored her until May of 1896, when they began surveilling her, and arrested her in August 1896. In the eight months between Lenin's imprisonment and Krupskaya's, they sent each other messages using "invisible" milk ink, a common communication strategy to avoid the prying eyes of the secret police in which a secret letter would be written in milk between the lines of an innocuous letter written in ink. The milk would dry and become "invisible." Because the chemicals in the milk weakened the paper, the milk ink would "develop" when the letter came into contact with heat and reveal the hidden message. Although political prisoners had no access to flames, they were often served tea hot enough to develop the invisible ink by holding the letter on or over the cup.

In addition to their hot tea and milk, political prisoners could receive unlimited visits from family members and from their spouses or fiancées. It is important to remember that many of these intellectual revolutionaries (including Lenin, Krupskaya, Kollontai, and Inessa Armand) hailed from the noble or bourgeois classes. The tsar perhaps saw them as angst-ridden youth rebelling against their high-status parents and dealt mildly with them, perhaps in hopes that they would grow out of their revolutionary zeal and eventually join their parents in the ranks of Russia's elite. Political prisoners were allowed visits from those to whom they were engaged and radicals in the Russian underground abused this fiancée provision to their own advantage, assigning fake fiancées to imprisoned men for the duration of their confinement. Krupskaya and other politically committed women volunteered for these roles and became couriers of messages, books, writing materials, and other necessities between prisoners and their conspirators. Between December 1895 and August 1896, Krupskaya became Vladimir Ilyich's political "fiancée."

Krupskaya's first imprisonment lasted from August to October of 1896. She was released, but then (rather impetuously) began raising money for a strike fund despite the fact that all strikes were illegal. The police arrested her again within weeks and she remained in jail until March of 1897, when her health deteriorated due to a thyroid condition that would plague her for the rest of her life. The government released Lenin in February 1897 and sentenced him to three years of exile in Siberia. At this time, Lenin sent Krupskaya a letter in invisible milk ink suggesting that if she too received a sentence of exile, she should join him as his "fiancée."

By early 1898, Krupskaya learned that she would also be sentenced to exile and agreed to go along with the plan. Lenin telegrammed the police to officially request that Krupskaya join him as his future spouse. Krupskaya wrote to the Ministry of Interior requesting the same, but as she was only exiled to a province in European Russia, she asked that one year of her sentence be reduced and that she be allowed to bring her mother. The police allowed her to go to Siberia for two years with Lenin, but on the condition that they marry as soon as she arrived (and she would still have to serve out her third year of exile in European Russia). Krupskaya and her mother set out for Siberia in April. Lenin and Krupskaya married in an Orthodox wedding ceremony in Shushenskoye in the summer of 1898.

Whatever the level of Lenin's romantic interest in Krupskaya, he certainly needed and appreciated her skills as a housewife and secretary. In addition to her work as a teacher, Krupskaya had been employed as a copyist, writing out duplications of documents for a railway company (as typewriters were rare). For all his revolutionary zeal, Lenin required domestic order and comfort; he also needed someone who could produce legible facsimiles of the many articles and books he used for research. One of the persistent criticisms of Bolshevik women's activists is that they rarely challenged traditional gender roles, especially in this early era. Although Kollontai openly criticized the persistence of the sexual double standard, in general socialists have tended to either ignore or reinforce a gendered division of labor. Enlightened socialist men (including those explicitly fighting for women's emancipation) had no problem relegating all of the necessary cooking or cleaning to their female comrades even when they recognized these tasks as tedious (remember the women snipers being asked to wash floors). Lenin explicitly addressed the stubbornness of male pride in a conversation with Clara Zetkin (although he was himself often complicit in this very problem): "So few men—even among the proletariat—realise how much effort and trouble they could save women, even quite do away with, if they were to lend a hand in 'women's work'. But no, that is contrary to the 'rights and dignity of a man'. They want their peace and comfort. The home life of the woman is a daily sacrifice to a thousand unimportant trivialities."[17]

Of course, these revolutionaries aspired to build a state wherein the "women's work" could be socialized, but until their future triumph, most Russian radicals relied on the status quo. After 1917, when Kollontai, Krupskaya, Armand, and the other women's activists in the Zhenotdel municipalized the laundries, opened public cafeterias, and built public nurseries and kindergartens, it was still overwhelmingly women who did the "women's work" (even if they now did it as state employees rather than housewives).[18] Although there would be later attempts to educate boys to help out more around the house and to encourage fathers to take a more active role in childrearing, in most cases collectivization, rather than a more equitable distribution of domestic work between men and women, remained the ultimate goal. This reality led to the infamous "double burden" that women workers faced.[19]

In *My Reminiscences of Lenin*, Krupskaya details the ways she facilitated Lenin's work by freeing him from domestic trifles. After their exile in Siberia, the couple settled in Munich in 1901. As Lenin began to write, Krupskaya became his nurse, cook, and therapist:

> I decided to put Vladimir Ilyich on home-cooked food and tackled the pots and pans. I did the cooking in the landlady's kitchen, but prepared everything in our own room. I tried to make as little noise as possible, because Vladimir Ilyich had then begun to write *What is to be done?* When writing, he would usually pace swiftly up and down the room, whispering what he was going to write. I had already adapted myself to his mode of working, and when he was writing I never spoke to him or asked him any questions. Afterwards, when we went out for a walk, he would tell me what he had written and what he was thinking about. This became as much a necessity to him as whispering his article over to himself before putting it down in writing.[20]

After the couple moved to London in 1902, Krupskaya also played the role of both doctor and nurse, diagnosing and arranging treatment when either her mother (who lived with them throughout their exile) or Lenin fell physically or psychologically ill. After a particularly trying conference, Lenin (prone to depression and anxiety) returned home under tremendous stress. Krupskaya reported: "Vladimir Ilyich's nerves were in such a bad state that he developed a nervous disease caused by the inflammation of the nerve endings of the back and chest. As soon as I saw the redness I looked up a medical handbook. I made it out to be ringworm ... and I painted Vladimir Ilyich with iodine, which caused him excruciating pain."[21] Years later, in Paris, Krupskaya recounted her troubles in setting up their new household in 1909:

> I had my hands full right away with all kinds of domestic cares. Household affairs had been much simpler in Geneva. Here it was a great bother. To get the gas connected I had to go up

to town three times before I received the necessary written order. The amount of red tape in France is unbelievable. To get books from the lending library you must have a householder to stand surety for you, and our landlord, seeing our miserable furniture, hesitated to do so. The housekeeping, too, at the beginning was a terrific bother.[22]

On top of all the care work she provided, Krupskaya faithfully toiled alongside Lenin in his political maneuvering against the Mensheviks and various other leftist factions attempting to dominate the Russian émigré communities in Western Europe. In her eulogy for Krupskaya, Kollontai explained, "When Lenin was forced to live long years in banishment abroad and guide the worker's Party from a distance, [Krupskaya] was not only his personal secretary but took the place of the whole staff of a Foreign Party Bureau as well."[23] From Krupskaya's memoir, we learn that Krupskaya edited the *Iskra* newspaper, smuggled literature into Russia, served as Lenin's chief cryptographer (enlisting her mother to write letters within which Krupskaya could embed secret messages in invisible ink), made contacts and found rooms for clandestine meetings, and prepared the reports and minutes of various socialist congresses. Having taught herself English, she translated articles about African colonialism into Russian while Lenin wrote *Imperialism* in Zurich in 1916.

Krupskaya also kept the accounting records, dealt with the finances, and organized communications between the émigré community and the underground in Russia, no small feat given the constant surveillance of mail by the tsarist police. To do this, she collected the addresses of sympathetic supporters in Western Europe who forwarded mail to the addresses of their supporters in Saint Petersburg, who then passed it on to activists in the underground. Her lists of good addresses proved invaluable in disseminating pro-Bolshevik newspapers in Russia before 1917, and her aptitude for logistics gave the Bolsheviks an edge over other less-well-organized émigré factions. As she had done in Saint Petersburg at her adult school, Krupskaya also gathered detailed information for Lenin from servant girls and workers, calling herself his "sedulous reporter."[24] On top of all this, she financially supported Lenin in Switzerland in the last years of their exile after her mother's death, eking out a spartan existence on a small sum she inherited from a "capitalist" aunt. While Lenin wrote, spoke, fulminated, and fomented, Krupskaya edited the copy, handled the post, paid the rent, and put food on the table. The life of the political exiles could be exciting—heated debates in dimly lit cafes, underground meetings, passionate speeches at large international congresses—but it could also be boring, tedious, and exhausting.

Krupskaya, the wizard of logistics, also labored over her own theories for a uniquely socialist pedagogy that would later serve as the bedrock for the global critical pedagogy movement. Still inspired by Tolstoy, and having honed her skills as a teacher among adult workers in Saint Petersburg, Krupskaya cultivated an insatiable curiosity about how educational systems functioned in Western democracies. In 1908, when Lenin and Krupskaya were living in Switzerland, she taught herself French and researched the organization of public education. She found in the Swiss schools the exact opposite of what she believed the children of workers needed to thrive in a future socialist society:

> I also began to study the system of school training in Geneva. I realized for the first time what a bourgeois school "for the people" was. I saw excellent buildings with lofty windows in which the children of workers were trained to be docile slaves. I saw the school-masters in one and the same classroom boxing the ears of workers' children and never touching the children of the rich. I saw how every child's mind was stifled of independent thought, how all learning was taught by cramming,

and how at every step the worship of power and wealth was inculcated in the children. I never imagined that anything of this kind could exist in a democratic country.[25]

Later in 1916, when they lived in Switzerland for the second time, Krupskaya again mentioned that she was "studying pedagogies" and familiarizing herself "with the practical side of the school system in Zurich."[26] Already familiar with the theories of Tolstoy and other Russian pedagogues, she acquainted herself with the ideas of many well-known educational reformers, including John Amos Comenius, Jean-Jacques Rousseau, Johan Heinrich Pestalozzi, Friedrich Fröbel, Robert Owen, Jane Addams, Maria Montessori, and John Dewey. Lenin hoped to cash in on Krupskaya's expansive knowledge of comparative educational systems by having her write a "pedagogical encyclopedia."[27] Krupskaya developed her ideas about the future of Soviet education in a 1918 essay, "Concerning the Question of Socialist Schools," which made clear references to her observations in Geneva:

In a bourgeois state—whether it is a monarchy or a republic—the school serves as an instrument for the spiritual enslavement of broad masses. Its objective in such a state is determined not by the interest of the pupils but by those of the ruling class, i.e. the bourgeoisie, and the interests of the two often differ quite substantially. The school's objective determines the entire organization of school activities, the entire structure of school life and the entire substance of school education.[28]

Krupskaya endeavored to completely reimagine the form, purpose, and content of the Russian educational system for both children and adults.

Between the February and October revolutions of 1917, Krupskaya busied herself with activities among the workers in the Vyborg district of the newly renamed Petrograd. She organized adult literacy courses in the factories, cleared land and built playgrounds for worker's children, and opened public reading rooms where citizens could access current newspapers, no doubt inspired by her time in émigré libraries. With the new rights to freedom of association granted by the Provisional Government, a variety of new youth organizations formed. Krupskaya involved herself with a pan-leftist group called "Light and Knowledge," which organized coeducational activities where little boys and little girls both learned their way around hammers and nails as well as needles and thread. She would later help create both the Komsomol and the Young Pioneers, two coeducational youth organizations theoretically designed to raise all boys and girls as equal, independent, and cooperative citizens of the workers' state.[29] If you wanted to promote women's equality with men, Krupskaya believed it best to start with the "small comrades" of the next generation.[30]

Krupskaya also hoped to form a children's union to advocate for the rights of child laborers (to a six-hour day, for instance) until such time that the Bolsheviks could abolish privately hired child labor completely. Instead, Krupskaya imagined a nationwide system of free, universal, and compulsory education for all children from ages seven to seventeen, which would include a work component following Marx's dictum that all children should participate in some manual labor as part of their preparation for socialist citizenship. And since parents would inevitably hold outdated traditional ideas about class and gender hierarchies, Krupskaya supported Kollontai's plans for children's homes and kindergartens where trained nurses and teachers would help raise them with a new set of socialist values which included sexual equality. If the bourgeoisie used public education to keep workers in their place, Krupskaya proposed using it to set them free. So where Kollontai supported socialized childcare to benefit Soviet women, Krupskaya argued that socialized childcare would also be good for the children.[31]

When the Bolsheviks seized power in October 1917, Krupskaya became the deputy minister in charge of adult education in the new Commissariat of Enlightenment (the Soviet name for the Ministry of Education), working together with the Ukrainian revolutionary Anatoly Lunacharsky.[32] Based on her understanding of progressive democratic pedagogies, Krupskaya began developing a program for large-scale educational reforms.[33] The new Soviet government proposed the first set of these reforms in 1919, and Krupskaya insisted on creating kindergartens and children's colonies for toddlers under the age of four as well as a system of special training schools for those over seventeen.[34] She had learned from her grassroots work in the Vyborg district in the summer of 1917 that workers "linked the revolutionary struggle with the struggle for mastering knowledge and culture," and wanted to promote a pedagogy which allowed them to combine these two aims.[35] Many peasants had lived off the land in a relatively non-monetized economy, but especially for peasants and workers who had recently migrated to the cities to take up factory jobs, becoming numerate allowed them to better

Nadezhda Krupskaya with Soviet workers

understand how employers cheated them of their wages. Similarly, learning to read gave workers access to a world of laws and regulations designed to protect them as well as to the newspapers and pamphlets striving to radicalize them.[36] Rather than learning to read from the Bible or from children's books, why not use *The Communist Manifesto*?

This new educational system required new books and lesson plans, and so Krupskaya also founded the field of Soviet librarianship.[37] Building on the workers' reading rooms set up before the war, Krupskaya helped to create a whole system of public libraries and reading rooms across the Soviet Union, even in the remotest of villages.[38] Peasants and workers had access to books and reading materials, and an army of specially trained librarians became the advanced guard of Soviet efforts to enlighten the masses. Krupskaya understood that books and the institutions that made them accessible were not politically neutral, and that the new workers' state required texts that ordinary citizens could relate to. Initially, though, she was opposed to the censorship of old books, even if they promoted reverence for the church and tsar. Otherwise austere, Krupskaya was a bibliophile who revered the classics.

During the chaos of the civil war, Krupskaya described a Red Army company which took over a school and "smashed up all of the appliances and tore the textbooks and exercise books to bits." The soldiers protested that the school and its books had belonged to the "master class" and needed to be destroyed along with all other vestiges of the former regime. Krupskaya also tells us that the workers' "thirst for knowledge was stronger than ever. [But] there were no textbooks to be had. The old textbooks with their prayers for the tsar and the Fatherland were destroyed by the Red Army men. They demanded textbooks that had a bearing on real life and on their own experiences."[39] Shifting her priorities to protect the new workers' state, Krupskaya signed three decrees between 1920 and 1924 that purged Russia's libraries of "counterrevolutionary" content. Although she did not author these decrees or produce the lists of banned books, she supported them based on her experiences of trying to educate illiterate Russian peasants. Compared with the workers—eager to learn and easy to radicalize—rural populations stubbornly clung to tradition.

Tolstoy once wrote: "The most difficult subjects can be explained to the most slow-witted man if he has not formed any idea of them already; but the simplest thing cannot be made clear to the most intelligent man if he is firmly persuaded that he knows already, without a shadow of doubt, what is laid before him."[40] In the realm of ideas, the forces of the old world dominated the written word, and Krupskaya may have been inspired by her previous idol. The "dangerous" texts included those on religion and non-Marxist philosophy as well as some literary fiction, poetry, and children's books (especially tales of the supernatural, including those involving anthropomorphized animals). Banned books were to be removed from the shelves and kept under lock and key in certain restricted sections of the library, to be used only by scholars and intellectuals for research purposes. In practice, many librarians refused these directives, but Krupskaya pushed for their enforcement and aligned herself with an intellectual censorship that she would have abhorred in her younger days.

Krupskaya's vision of the ideal Soviet education system was a decentralized and liberal one, with local teachers forming unions that would help run the schools. She resisted the idea of a centralized authority. Her educational proposals (emerging in part from her youthful interlude as a Tolstoyan) also devolved authority from the teacher to the students themselves. This would foster an educational environment where students would have individual agency to shape and direct their own learning. Krupskaya wrote in 1918: "The most important distinguishing feature of socialist schools should be that their only objective is the pupil's fullest possible and most comprehensive development. They must not suppress his individuality but only help develop it. Socialist schools are schools of freedom in which there is no room for regimentation, rote learning and cramming."[41] In her view, socialist education would promote intellectual and emotional autonomy, not so different from the ideals of progressive educators in the West.

Krupskaya committed to a vision of a "polytechnical" education, one that combined the individual development of students with a program for their social and political development as workers and citizens.[42] Krupskaya considered "monotechnic" education (what we might call vocational schools where students learn a specific trade) a tool of the bourgeois to keep the working classes in their place. Lunacharsky supported Krupskaya's plan for a polytechnical pedagogy, but, as with Kollontai's vision of socialized care work, Krupskaya's plan ran afoul of Soviet realities. With the Soviet economy in shambles, Lenin himself insisted that the new country needed workers skilled in specific trades, such as metal workers, lathe operators, and mechanical engineers. It could not afford the lofty goals of what we might think of as a "labor arts" education for all Soviet children. Rather than learning just one set of specific skills, Krupskaya imagined a system in which students learned the basics of many types of work and the general aptitudes that they had in common. As a compromise, Lenin proposed supplementing vocational lessons with courses on Marxism and the history of the Communist Party, not even a pale shadow of Krupskaya's original vision.

Later, Stalin rejected the idea of an educational system which might produce free-thinking and independent Soviet citizens; he needed cogs in his big modernization wheel. Under his leadership, Soviet schools returned to lessons based on recitation and memorization (exactly what Krupskaya most criticized about bourgeois education in Geneva). Full disciplinary authority returned to teachers, and the education system was centralized. Supplemental lessons on dialectical materialism turned into little more than state propaganda taught through drills and exams. Although the Soviets never fully embraced Krupskaya's ideas for a unique socialist pedagogy, her theories did prove an essential foundation for later radical educators. When the Brazilian Paulo Freire, a great twentieth-century proponent of critical pedagogy, began investigating the ideal relationship between student and teacher, he drew inspiration from Krupskaya's work.[43] She dreamed of an educational system wherein teachers would serve as mere facilitators: intellectual midwives for independent thoughts and ideas. The truly liberatory potential of Krupskaya's pedagogical vision is perhaps best confirmed by Stalin's total rejection of it.[44]

Unlike Kollontai's personal life, which was filled with passion and drama, Krupskaya's remained subdued. She and Lenin never had children (possibly due to her thyroid condition) and witnesses claimed that she slept in her mother's room rather than in her husband's while they lived in exile.[45] After the revolution, they often lived apart, and Krupskaya became Lenin's regular companion again only when he needed an attentive nurse: first after he was shot at close range by Fanny Kaplan on August 30, 1918, and later·after he suffered from a series of increasingly debilitating strokes.

Krupskaya's most affectionate relationship was with Inessa Armand. The most tender and evocative language in her memoir appears not in passages about Lenin or her mother, but when she describes time shared with Armand, whom she first met in France. The 1910 Paris crowd included Alexandra Kollontai and Alexander Shlyapnikov; Armand began attending the talks and events organized by the Russian émigré community. "Inessa Armand arrived in Paris from Brussels in 1910 and immediately became an active member of our Paris group," Krupskaya wrote. "She was elected to the presidium of the group and started an extensive correspondence with the other groups abroad. She had a family of two little girls and a boy. She was a hot Bolshevik, and before long our whole Paris crowd had gathered around her."[46]

During this time, Krupskaya, Lenin, and Armand decided to organize a summer school in the village of Longjumeau, near Paris. Armand rented a house, which served as a canteen for students who rented rooms in the village. Krupskaya recalls fondly that she and Lenin rented rooms in a brick house at the other end of the village, but always dined in the common room at Armand's place, where they enjoyed long conversations with the students. When Lenin and Krupskaya moved back to Paris in 1910, after the summer, Armand rented the apartment right next to theirs and saw them almost every day. After leaving Paris, Lenin and Krupskaya settled in Cracow/ Kraków (in Austrian Poland) with Krupskaya's mother, who was ill. Armand eventually joined them after serving a harsh prison sentence in Russia. Much to Krupskaya's surprise, Armand arrived ready to labor: "She had lost none of her old energy, however, and threw herself into party work with all her usual zest."[47] Krupskaya waxed lyrical about their months together:

> That autumn all of us—our entire Cracow group—were drawn very close to Inessa. She was just brimming with vitality and exuberant good spirits. We had known her in Paris, but the colony there had been a large one, whereas in Cracow we lived together in a small close and friendly circle. Inessa rented a room in the same house where Kamenev lived. My mother was greatly attached to her. Inessa often came to have a chat with her, or sit and smoke. Things seemed cosier and more cheerful when Inessa was there.
>
> Our home life was more like that of students, and we were very glad to have Inessa. During this visit of hers, she told me a great deal about her life and her children, and showed me their

letters. There was a delightful warmth about her stories. Ilyich and I went for long walks with Inessa.[48]

After the beginning of World War I and Lenin's arrest in Poland, Krupskaya and Lenin fled to Switzerland. Armand decided to join them for several months. From Krupskaya's descriptions of their time in Berne, it seems the trio spent many happy hours in each other's company:

> That autumn is associated in my mind with the colorful picture of the Berne woods. It was a lovely autumn that year. In Berne we lived in Distelweg, a clean, quiet little street adjoining the Berne woods, which stretched for several miles. Inessa lived across the road ... We used to roam for hours along the woodland paths, which were bestrewn with yellow leaves. Mostly the three of us went on these walks together—Vladimir Ilyich, Inessa, and myself. Vladimir Ilyich spoke about his plans of struggle along international lines. Inessa was very enthusiastic about it all. She had begun to take a direct part in the rising struggle—she carried on correspondence, translated various of our documents into French and English, collected material, talked with people, etc. Sometimes we would sit for hours on a sunny wooded hillside, Ilyich jotting down notes for his articles and speeches, and polishing his formulations, I studying Italian with the aid of a Toussaint textbook, and Inessa sewing a skirt and basking in the autumn sunshine—she had not quite recovered yet from the effects of her imprisonment.[49]

Krupskaya briefly mentioned moments when she and Armand shared time alone together without Lenin—when they searched for rooms in Cracow or visited a comrade in the hospital. Their personal letters make clear that the two women shared a strong personal as well as political bond and raise some interesting possibilities. Robert McNeal, one of Krupskaya's biographers, also found the relationship between the two women atypical:

The Inessa-Lenin-Krupskaya triangle poses a number of riddles that can neither be fully solved nor simply ignored in a life of Krupskaya. For one thing, it *was* a triangle, not just a "V" formed by one person's relationship with two others, as in so many alleged triangles. In time, at least, there was a close personal bond between Inessa and Krupskaya, as well as between Inessa and Lenin.[50]

Krupskaya personally edited a special volume of tributes after Armand's death in 1920, and she essentially adopted two of Armand's younger children, caring for them as if they were her own.[51]

If Krupskaya's initial betrothal and ultimate marriage to Lenin occurred for the sake of politics, it is not unreasonable to ask whether the two ever shared a romantic life together, especially after their initial "honeymoon" in Siberian exile. Could it have been a ménage à trois? This seems doubtful, given that Krupskaya seemed rather constrained in her sexual mores. Perhaps Krupskaya had committed to leading a dedicated, ascetic life like her youthful role models Tolstoy and the fictional Rakhmetov. Or maybe she harbored a secret love for Inessa, or openly cultivated a "passionate friendship," a not uncommon arrangement among Victorian women of her time (and not so different from the relationship between Kollontai and Shadurskaya).[52]

As both Vivian Gornick and Maple Razsa have described in their work on communist and anarchist movements, romance has played a large role in drawing individuals into revolutionary causes.[53] "Powerful feelings of camaraderie, commonality, loyalty, solidarity—even love for one another and the collective —are a critical part of radical political experience, born of shared struggle," writes Razsa. "In some cases, these experiences are at the very emotional center of individual motivation and inspiration."[54] If you fall in love with a struggle, it is easy to fall in love with those who share that struggle and vice versa.

After Lenin's death in January 1924, Krupskaya found herself caught in the political vacuum and internecine struggles that accompanied the scramble for power. At great personal risk, she smuggled Lenin's "last testament" out of Russia so that Max Eastman could publish it in the *New York Times* in 1926, but Lenin's negative assessments of Stalin failed to penetrate the censorship in the Soviet Union.[55] Krupskaya could do nothing to prevent Stalin's ascension. Never a fan of the Georgian, whom she considered rude and unsophisticated, she pushed back against Stalin's policies as often as she could.[56] We catch a fascinating glimpse of the widow Krupskaya in 1928 when she delivered a keynote address to the Fourth All-Union Zhenotdel Conference of Party Organizers Among Eastern Women in Moscow. At the time, Stalin and the women of the Zhenotdel were engaged in a top-down campaign to liberate the women of Soviet Central Asia, whom Gregory Massell calls "the surrogate proletariat." Krupskaya thought this heavy-handed form of forced emancipation would backfire and harm the long-term prospects for building communism among the Muslim populations. Reflecting on Krupskaya's speech, Massell writes:

> While Krupskaia's address was for the most part cautiously worded, and was replete with vaguely assenting references to the current party line, its crucial segments bore all the marks of an intellectual and moral crisis. Lenin's widow in effect rejected some of the most important premises underlying the notion of a revolution from above. She rejected a revolution by administrative command, especially when it involved a sweeping, dogmatic, and ruthless assault on human communities and sensibilities. Hers was, quite obviously, a plea for gradualism, and for toleration of a modicum of social and cultural pluralism. It was an urgent plea for respect for, and sensitive adaptation to, local conditions and peculiarities.[57]

Krupskaya's words had little effect in changing Stalinist policy, and she was isolated and persecuted by Stalin and other party members willing to do his bidding. Trotsky recalled, after her death:

> She made an attempt to oppose the Stalinist clique and in 1926 found herself for a brief interval in the ranks of the Opposition. Frightened by the prospect of a split, she broke away. Having lost confidence in herself, she completely lost her bearings, and the ruling clique did everything in their power to break her morally. On the surface she was treated with respect, or rather with semi-honors. But within the apparatus itself she was systematically discredited ... and subjected to indignities.[58]

Nikita Khrushchev also recollected that the rank and file turned against Krupskaya after she tried once more to oppose Stalin in May 1930. "Without any publicity the word went out to the party cells to give her a working-over. She was

Nadezhda Krupskaya in the 1930s

avoided like the plague ... was kept under close surveillance ... everyone was slinging mud at Nadezhda Konstaninovna."[59]

In the 1930s, Krupskaya watched Stalin purge and murder her Old Bolshevik comrades, trying to intercede where she could. Like Kollontai, she eventually accommodated herself to Stalin's rule while dealing with her own deteriorating health. "Stalin always lived in fear of a protest on her part," Trotsky wrote in 1939:

> She knew far too much. She knew the history of the party. She knew the place that Stalin occupied in this history. All of the latter day historiography which assigned to Stalin a place alongside of Lenin could not but appear revolting and insulting to her. Stalin feared Krupskaya just as he feared Gorky. Krupskaya was surrounded ... Her old friends disappeared one by one; those who delayed in dying were murdered either openly or secretly. Every step she took was supervised. Her articles appeared in the press only after interminable, insufferable and degrading negotiations between the censors and the author ... What recourse was there for the unfortunate crushed woman? Completely isolated, a heavy stone weighing upon her heart, uncertain what to do, in the toils of sickness, she dragged on her burdensome existence.[60]

Whereas Kollontai capitulated to Stalin from the safety of her diplomatic mission in Stockholm, Krupskaya lived next door to him, surrounded by his spies, wounded by his slanders, and forced to compromise her ideals. She died in February 1939. Stalin gave her a state funeral and even helped carry her urn to the Kremlin wall, but minimized remembrances of her so he would have no competition as the keeper of Lenin's legacy. After Nikita Khrushchev's secret speech in 1956 (exposing the horrors of Stalin's rule), the new Soviet premier resuscitated her memory as part of his de-Stalinization campaign. Krupskaya's life and work were widely celebrated in the Soviet Union, and many of her books and articles reprinted. Between 1970 and 1992, the Soviet Union sponsored the UNESCO Nadezhda K. Krupskaya Literacy Prize,[61] and to this day Russians can still savor a domestically produced Krupskaya chocolate bar.[62] Through Krupskaya's work with youth groups, particularly the Young Pioneers, she touched the lives of millions of children, and although childless herself, came to be viewed as a maternal figure for the whole of the Soviet Union.

But her most enduring legacy was her utter devotion to the revolution and her unique vision of a liberatory socialist pedagogy. As one prominent American labor leader, Louis Segal, wrote in 1939: "She was a woman of the rarest sincerity and entirely devoted to the man and the cause she had espoused. No task was too mean and no work was too difficult so long as it advanced the cause which was dear to her."[63]

4

The "Hot Bolshevik"

Inessa Armand (1874–1920)

Of the troika of Red Valkyries involved in agitating for the Bolshevik revolution and laying the groundwork for their unique brand of socialist women's activism in the early years of the Union of Soviet Socialist Republics, Inessa Armand remains the most enigmatic. Unlike Alexandra Kollontai and Nadezhda Krupskaya, who both survived Lenin's death and Stalin's purges, Armand died in 1920 at the age of forty-six. Kollontai and Krupskaya lived long enough to write many articles and give many speeches, and both wrote extensive memoirs. Armand wrote fewer of her own articles and essays and the story of her life is mostly known through her letters, not all of which have survived. Krupskaya wrote some of the most vivid portraits of Armand in her memoir about Lenin, and Krupskaya prepared the 1926 edited volume of commemorative essays for her dear friend.

Two additional and related factors muddle Inessa Armand's story. First, it seems that historians in the Soviet government intentionally altered facts about her life to make it conform with their ideal of how a Bolshevik revolutionary and close associate of Lenin should have lived. Western scholars who used these Soviet sources during the Cold War often unknowingly reproduced these distortions.[1] For example, Inessa Armand was raised in the solidly middle-class household of her Russian grandmother after her parents' death. Soviet biographers claim she came to Russia as the ward of an aunt who served as the governess of the wealthy Armand family,

Inessa Armand and her five children in 1909

and that this family generously allowed her to be educated with their own children. Furthermore, after her marriage to the wealthy and bourgeois Alexander Armand, she often received funds from him to support her revolutionary work, a fact elided by Soviet sources. And when Inessa Armand began an intimate relationship with her husband's younger brother, Vladimir, one biographer suggested that Vladimir was only one year younger than Inessa. In reality, she was twenty-eight and he was eighteen when they started their affair.

Second, circumstantial evidence suggests that Lenin and Armand were very close friends, lovers, two sides of a revolutionary love triangle with Krupskaya, or all of the above. But much of this evidence rests on hearsay from associates of Armand including Alexandra Kollontai and Angelica Balabanova, as well as the Soviet decision to suppress a certain subset of Lenin's personal letters until after the collapse of communism in 1991. Krupskaya's English biographer, Robert McNeal, asserts that Alexandra Kollontai's 1923 novella, "A Great Love," is a thinly fictionalized account of the relationship between Lenin, Krupskaya, and Armand.[2] Western scholars of this so-called romantic school make much of the fact than Lenin addressed Armand with the informal *ty* pronoun in Russian rather that the more formal *vy* for a certain period of time.³ Lenin rarely used this pronoun outside of his immediate family, and the content of the letters hint that Lenin and Armand may have indulged in at least a summer fling, although some biographers insist otherwise.⁴ The topic was, and remains a sensitive one: the Soviet government ordered the Moscow bureau of *Time* magazine closed after it ran an April 1964 cover story which mentioned a "ménage à trois" in the Lenin household.⁵ The rumors and insinuations about the affair overshadowed her significant contributions to the socialist women's movements and the Bolshevik revolution. Of the two English-language biographies of Armand, one bears the title *Lenin's Mistress*, as if this single romantic relationship (if it happened) was the defining characteristic of her life.⁶

Like Lenin and Krupskaya, Armand adored Nikolai Chernyshevsky's novel *What Is to Be Done?*, but rather than following the example of the celibate Rakhmetov, she lived a life not so dissimilar from the emancipated protagonist, Vera Pavlovna. In the book, a character called Lopukhov marries Vera Pavlovna to liberate her from the loveless marriage being forced upon her by her unsympathetic mother. But when Vera Pavlovna later falls in love with Lopukhov's best friend, Kirsanov, Lopukhov fakes his own suicide with the help of Rakhmetov and leaves for the United States so that Vera Pavlovna and Kirsanov can marry. Armand's real life mirrored this story. She married Alexander Armand and bore him four children, but, when she became pregnant by Vladimir Armand (Alexander's younger, radical brother), Alexander allowed her to be with Vladimir. Alexander eschewed jealousy and the bothersome process of divorce, and continued to pay for tutors, governesses, and schools for all five children while he and Inessa remained married, freeing Inessa to pursue her own education and political career in exile.

That all of this happened in 1903 might seem shocking to those among us who consider polyamory a phenomenon of relatively recent and Western vintage. But leftists often challenged the amorous status quo as part of their progressive politics. Friedrich Engels lived in a throuple with Mary Burns and her sister Lizzie for years until Mary's death, after which he continued to live with Lizzie and even married her at the end of her life.[7] In fin de siècle tsarist Russia, too, Chernyshevsky's book and the general zeitgeist of the time inspired many writers, artists, and intellectuals to question the strict social mores of bourgeois culture, particularly the often-stultifying chains of monogamous marriage. Most famously, the futurist poet Vladimir Mayakovsky lived in an open ménage à trois with Osip and Lilya Brik between 1915 and 1930.[8] Inessa and the Armand brothers seemed to embody the spirit of what Kollontai had tried to capture in her essay "Make Way for Winged Eros," questioning why love should require an exclusive property relationship between two people, and why people should not strive to overcome jealousy as they resist other basic feelings that compel them to behave in ways they abhor.

Born in Paris, Inessa Fyodorovna Armand (née Elisabeth-Ines Stéphane d'Herbenville) grew up in Russia with her aunt and grandmother after her parents' early deaths. Her father was a French opera singer and her mother was an actress; the two married after Inessa's mother became pregnant with her. Inessa enjoyed a solid middle-class education, spoke several languages, and played the piano quite well. At nineteen, she married Alexander, the son of a well-to-do French-Russian family that owned textile mills just outside of Saint Petersburg. The Armands were politically liberal but solidly bourgeois and Inessa's conjugal life was very comfortable by late-nineteenth-century Russian standards. In the first six years of her marriage, she bore four children, but, as with Kollontai, the expectations for women of Armand's class bored her. Philanthropic work offered an acceptable distraction, and, unlike Kollontai and Krupskaya, Armand counted herself among the ranks of the feminists before she joined the socialists.

In 1899, Inessa Armand helped found the Moscow Society for Improving the Lot of Women. She served briefly as the chair of its education commission and accepted its presidency in 1900, a post she held for three years. A nascent feminist organization, the Moscow Society promoted education and technical training for women and girls. Armand attempted to organize Sunday schools and a feminist journal, but the tsarist authorities refused to grant her permission, fearing that women's rights provided a front for more nefarious anti-autocratic activities. Undeterred, Armand applied for permission to organize a "Shelter for Downtrodden Women" in 1902, aimed at rehabilitating what Russians at the turn of the twentieth century called *"prostitutki"* and preventing illiterate

Inessa Armand in 1895

teenage girls from the countryside from joining the ranks of the oldest profession. Recall that Russian life expectancy in 1900 was only thirty years and living standards for the peasantry after the abolition of serfdom were deteriorating.[9] Peasant girls were not empowered women freely choosing a vocation that bourgeois society disparaged; they were hungry and desperate teens who had fled grueling rural poverty to find factory work in the city, where the abysmal wages forced them to sell sex to survive.

The authorities granted permission for the women's shelter, and Armand and her feminist colleagues tried to help the girls find jobs at living wages. Armand worked in the Moscow Society for four years, but quickly became disillusioned with the obstructionism of the tsarist government and the difficulties of running the shelter. When the paranoid bureaucracy blocked other purely philanthropic feminist activities, Armand accepted that only political change would help women. Industrialization had overturned feudalism but capitalism provided the former serfs with few opportunities to make a decent living. Through her work at the shelter, Armand discovered the structural roots of the economic coercion that forced women onto the streets after a full day's labor in the factories.

The labor laws, such as they existed at the time, heavily favored employers. An 1882 law, for instance, prohibited the employment of children under the age of twelve, and limited the working time of children between the ages of twelve and fourteen to eight hours a day. But from the age of fifteen, the workday could extend from fourteen to eighteen hours and still not provide enough pay for even basic sustenance.[10] Even worse, employers could dismiss workers at their leisure and impose fines for any variety of infractions; a worker could lose a day's wages for being just five minutes late. Employers could decide to pay their laborers in kind or force them to shop at the factory store where inflated prices pushed the workers into debt. These debts rendered it difficult for workers to seek new employment, and their illiteracy made it impossible to seek legal recourse (if there was any to be had). If workers attempted to organize to improve their conditions, they were fined, harassed, or imprisoned for strikes and other industrial actions.

Armand, like many well-meaning ladies of her social class, initially imagined that charity work could help alleviate the plight of working-class women. For the members of the "upper ten thousand," philanthropy provided an acceptable social life outside of the domestic sphere. When they encountered obstacles or frustration, they could retreat to the comfortable drawing rooms of their country estates, secure in the knowledge that they had not completely ignored the trials of those less fortunate than themselves. But Armand grew angry at the system. Receptive to new ideas and unwilling to give up her fight for Russian women, she turned away from the feminists. Government obstinacy and elite callousness pushed her into the arms of more radical elements of Russian society.

These radical elements took the form of her seventeen-year-old brother-in-law, Vladimir, whom she had known since childhood. He had moved to Moscow to study at the university and they often shared an apartment owned by the Armand family. Because of her work with the Moscow Society, Armand spent many days away from her husband. Alexander, who held various important positions in Russian society, also spent considerable time away from Armand on business and the pair began to grow apart. Vladimir introduced Armand to Marx, Engels, and other writers developing a critique of the capitalist system. He held student meetings and exposed Armand to a network of young people dreaming of a different future for Russia.

When Armand and Vladimir took a holiday to Italy in 1903, she returned pregnant with her fifth child. Between 1903 and 1908, Armand became increasingly active in revolutionary meetings and activities in Moscow, smuggling illegal Marxist literature into Russia and running a clandestine library (her base in Moscow explains why, in this early period, her work did not overlap with that of Kollontai or Krupskaya, who were based in St. Petersburg). Hounded by the authorities, she spent considerable time in jail, including an extended period of exile in the far northern city of Mezen just below the Arctic Circle. Vladimir voluntarily followed Armand into exile (just as Krupskaya had followed Lenin) even though the brutal cold exacerbated his already poor health. The small town of Mezen bulged with political exiles from across the empire, living together in poor conditions. In February of 1908, Armand wrote to Alexander:

> We are getting by as usual, the same dull life: the days don't pass but somehow imperceptibly slide by like pale bloodless shadows. As much as we can, we deceive ourselves, then try to convince others ... that there is life here. Of course, I am better off than the others because I am not alone. Many others are completely alone and they are having a bad time of it. On the other hand, I am worse off than the others because there, in Moscow, are the children whom I miss and worry about.[11]

Armand always struggled with what we would call work–family balance, constantly juggling the demands of the revolution with the emotional needs of her two daughters, three sons, two de facto husbands, and possibly a lover and his wife. In 1908, she wrote to a friend: "The friction between personal and family interests [on the one hand] and societal interests [on the other] is one of the most serious problems facing the intelligentsia today."[12] From Mezen she penned numerous letters pleading with the authorities to let her live in Archangel where she could see her children. The authorities refused every time. Her extended stints in solitary confinement caused her own health to falter. A woman with less tenacity would have given up.

When Vladimir became too ill to stay with her in Mezen, he left for the south of France and Armand plotted her escape. A group of Polish exiles who had received permission to leave Mezen agreed to smuggle her out. Armand first made her way to Moscow, then stopped briefly in Saint Petersburg to listen in on the Women's Congress, where delegates debated the possibilities for women's emancipation and the future of marriage. She stayed among the crowds in the galleries to hide from the tsarist police (Kollontai was also hiding there) but listened to the discussions with great interest. In a letter to Vladimir, she wrote, "There is a contradiction in life. On the one hand there are yearnings for freedom to love, and on the other women presently have so paltry an income that for the majority of them this freedom is unattainable or they must remain childless."[13] Armand understood that her ability to engage in political activism was borne of her privilege. While she fled the authorities, Alexander provided her money and organized care for her children, perhaps as much because he loved her as out of sympathy for her cause. Few women had husbands willing or able to support the political dreams of their wives.

Armand planned to hide out in Kiev, but when she received word that Vladimir's health was failing, she illegally crossed the border into Finland. She rushed to the French Riviera only to find her lover in the grip of advanced tuberculosis, perhaps worsened by his time with her in Mezen. In early 1909, Vladimir died in Armand's arms. Devastated by her loss, she went to stay with Alexander and her children in Roubaix, France, where Alexander had relocated with two of their sons after receiving his own sentence of exile from Russia. After Roubaix, Inessa spent some time alone in Paris, grieving and trying to grope her way into the future. Wanted in Russia for her escape from Mezen, she had no choice but to stay in Western Europe. It was in Paris that Armand was introduced to the city's Russian émigré community. At a political

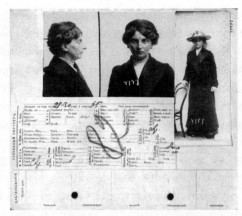

Inessa Armand's registration cards in the Samara Province in 1912

meeting on the second floor of the Café Les Manilleurs, Inessa Armand first met Vladimir Lenin and Nadezhda Krupskaya.[14]

Alexander convinced Armand to take a comfortable holiday with him and the children and she agreed, no doubt needing time to recuperate her physical and mental health. After their vacation, Alexander invited her to return to Roubaix for the remainder of his exile, perhaps hoping for a reconciliation. But Armand had other aspirations. She understood that the West European Social Democrats, socialists, communists, and anarchists respected theorists. Rosa Luxemburg, Alexandra Kollontai and other women like them had made a place for themselves in the movement by studying Marxism and writing and publishing theoretical texts. Armand chose to live in Brussels, and (with Alexander's continued financial support) enrolled in the Université Nouvelle (near Roubaix) where she started a two-year course in economic sciences, submerging herself in her studies while also caring for her three younger children. After only ten months, she sat the exams and earned her certificate in July of 1910. While in Belgium, she also worked occasionally with the local Russian Social Democratic organization and helped forward newspapers and other party publications sent from Paris on to Russia.

Shortly after she finished her course, Armand traveled to Copenhagen to attend the Second International Conference of Socialist Women in August 1910. She had been exiled in Mezen for the First International Conference of Socialist Women in Stuttgart in 1907, but she had read the protocols and knew that the key debates would revolve around whether socialist women should support bourgeois feminists and the demands for either limited or universal suffrage. Clara Zetkin dominated the proceedings on behalf of the women of the German Social Democratic Party. It was at this conference in Copenhagen where Zetkin famously proposed that "socialist women in each country shall organize, in agreement with the political workers' parties and trade unions, a special Women's Day"[15] which formed the basis of the International Women's Day still globally celebrated on March 8.[16] It was also in Copenhagen that Inessa Armand gained inspiration from Zetkin's women's newspaper, *Die Gleichheit* ("Equality"), which eventually led to the short-lived Russian working women's paper *Rabotnitsa* ("Woman Worker").[17] After the women's congress concluded, Armand attended the eighth Congress of the Socialist International in Copenhagen, where she exchanged views with Lenin, Trotsky, Luxemburg, and other luminaries of the European socialist movement and, after her crash course in economics in Brussels, discovered a renewed commitment to Marxism. She moved from Brussels to Paris with her three younger children but, after the end of Alexander's exile, all of her children returned with him to Russia. On her own in France, Armand became a regular member of Lenin and Krupskaya's inner Bolshevik circle, a disciplined foot soldier of the vanguard party.

In the Karl Marx museum in Trier, Germany, I once bought a print of a diagram called "The Family Tree of Socialism." The tree with its many roots provides a wonderful visualization of all of the various workers' movements that influenced twentieth-century communism. Karl Kautsky and Eduard Bernstein created it in 1896 for the fourth annual congress of the Second International, in an attempt to map out how all earlier varieties of progressive thought fused into the works of Marx and Engels and would inevitably lead to international unity and the "May Day of the Proletariat."[18] But theoretical unity among the left remains as elusive today as it was in 1896 when the diagram was made. The texts of Marx and Engels left ample room for different interpretations and each self-styled socialist theorist fashioned their own exegetical interpretation of the "correct" way to forge a path out of capitalism. Disagreements and factionalism have characterized socialist movements since their inception.

For Lenin, Krupskaya, and other Bolsheviks, consolidating the working-class movement around the revolutionary struggle often put them in direct conflict with Social Democrats who preferred an electoral path to power. The Bolsheviks believed that reform and small concessions to the proletariat diffused the militancy required for class struggles. Lenin and Krupskaya spent much of their time in exile fighting with other socialists. Here, Inessa Armand became Lenin's invaluable deputy. To start, he tasked her with the organization of a special party summer school outside of Paris in 1911, the same school where Lenin and Krupskaya shared their meals with Armand every night. The school would train a new generation of disciplined Bolsheviks who would support Lenin at the various socialist congresses. With Alexander's financial assistance, Armand rented a two-story house in the small French town of Longjumeau, where she lived throughout the summer with her seven-year-old son, Andrei. Lenin apparently trusted Armand with all of the practicalities of running the school. The first floor of her house served as the kitchen and communal dining room for all of the students, many of whom arrived from Russia. Armand proved a gracious hostess and Krupskaya later reported that "the comradely atmosphere which was created was to a remarkable extent the work of Inessa."[19] Armand also lectured at the school on the history of Belgian socialism.

In September, when Lenin and Krupskaya returned to Paris, Armand followed them. Her two daughters joined her from Russia, and she lived in the apartment next door to Lenin and Krupskaya with her three younger children. Together, the three adults and three children lived in a kind of communal pod, and it was during the next nine months that, as Krupskaya writes, "Inessa became very close to us." They organized, fundraised, and plotted to unite Europe's various socialist movements under one Leninist banner of Bolshevism, which created many enemies for them in Paris, where his dogmatic views found few adherents. Lenin eventually decided to move his headquarters to Cracow, then in the Austrian section of partitioned Poland and much closer to Russia.

Armand soon quit Paris as well, and Lenin dispatched her on a mission back to Russia. She was still wanted by the authorities for her escape from Mezen in 1909 and returning home therefore entailed considerable personal risk, but she went anyway. The tsar's police arrested her, and she spent six months from 1912 to 1913 in solitary confinement in a pre-trial prison in Saint Petersburg. When her health began to fail and she showed early symptoms of tuberculosis, Alexander (still her legal husband) convinced the authorities to release his wife to his custody against an enormous bail of 5,400 rubles and a promise that she would appear at her trial. Forced by circumstance to give up her work for Lenin and the Bolsheviks, Armand spent the spring and summer with Alexander and her children on a lavish holiday trip down the Volga River and to Stavropol and the Caucuses, sharing time with her children, and possibly reconnecting with her husband. Alexander, for his part, had no wish to see Armand return to jail or be sent again to exile. The night before her trial in late August 1913, Armand snuck over the border into

Finland, costing her poor husband an elephantine sum of money when he had to forfeit the bail.

Armand made her way to Cracow and lived for a while within the small Bolshevik community, once again finding cozy relations with her comrades, particularly Krupskaya and her mother. But Lenin overburdened Armand with endless translation work, and she returned to Paris in December 1913, where she spearheaded the publication of the women's journal *Rabotnitsa*. The first attempt by socialists to reach out to the working women of Russia, *Rabotnitsa*'s inaugural issue appeared on International Women's Day in 1914. Although the print run was small (12,000 copies, barely enough to distribute throughout Saint Petersburg where there was a higher concentration of literate women), Armand, Krupskaya, and their colleagues managed to publish seven issues between March and June 1914. The tsarist police seized the print runs of three of these issues and publication efforts abruptly stopped with the breakout of World War I. Although short-lived, *Rabotnitsa* provided a foundation for the socialist women's movement in Russia and was resurrected soon after the abdication of the tsar in 1917.

Whatever the nature of their relationship, Lenin abused the talents and patience of Armand to an extraordinary degree. He proved both demanding and ungrateful when he asked Armand to continue to work for him in Paris in early 1914, and she was probably happy to decamp to the Adriatic coast for a much-needed vacation with her younger children in May of that year. Armand's children missed their mother (her youngest son, Andrei, was already ten by 1914, and her daughters were teenagers), and she hoped to relax with them during the summer months. Andrei was ill, and Armand felt compelled to set political work aside for her family and to enjoy some well-earned repose.

By early July, Lenin had sent four letters begging Armand to leave her children and attend a so-called "Unity" congress in Brussels. The German Social Democrats wanted to unite the various Russian émigré factions so they could act more effectively. As usual, Lenin was in no mood for conciliation and his stubbornness had drawn the ire of his German comrades. For strategic reasons, Lenin needed someone else to deliver his statement, and his top male Bolshevik colleagues refused to attend on his behalf (perhaps realizing how unpopular Lenin's position would be). Only after Lenin's repeated insistence did Armand finally agree to represent the Bolsheviks at the congress which opened on July 16, 1914. She left her children at the seaside, and begrudgingly made her way to Belgium. There, she faced an avalanche of criticism and approbation from the other delegates when she presented Lenin's ultimatum: that unity was only possible if all Russian factions united under the authority of the Bolsheviks. Armand faced immense ridicule for being a "Leninist," but the delegates knew that there could be no unity without him. When the congress ended, Lenin instructed Armand to visit him in Poland before returning to her children on the Adriatic coast. She flat out refused, instead resuming her holiday and making plans to travel back to the Russian border with her children. For this disobedience, Lenin ceased to address his letters to Armand using the informal pronoun *ty*. Armand had declared her independence just as the Great Powers of Europe declared war.

The outbreak of World War I created a massive chasm between those who supported nationalist war efforts in the name of defense and those who clung to the principles of proletarian internationalism. Like the Germans, the French socialists embraced the narrative of national defense, and abandoned the idea that the workers of the world would unite. Armand firmly sided with Lenin in his call for civil war. After she safely returned her children to Russia, she traveled to Switzerland. Lenin had been arrested in Austrian Poland, and it was Armand who raised the necessary money to fund

Lenin's and Krupskaya's travel to Bern upon his release. For a while, Lenin, Krupskaya, and Armand lived near each other in Bern, often going for the long autumn walks that Krupskaya describes so fondly in her memoir. But toward the end of 1914, Armand decided that she wanted to write a theoretical pamphlet on love, marriage, and the family. Perhaps inspired by the writings of Zetkin and Kollontai—and hoping to make use of her education in Brussels—Armand left Bern for several weeks of solitude in the Swiss mountains to draft her pamphlet. Given her own unorthodox personal experiences with Alexander and Vladimir, she probably wrote a fascinating treatise on women's right to choose their partners based on love rather than social convention or economic necessity. Unfortunately, she sent her first draft to Lenin for comments. He hated it and told her so. Armand apparently defended herself against his criticisms in a now lost letter, and he replied with even more disparaging words, belittling her and blaming her for "completely forgetting the objective and class point of view."[20] Armand never published her pamphlet, and no copy of it remains.

Lenin kept Armand busy with party work between 1915 and 1917, sending her to represent the Bolsheviks at both youth and women's congresses where Lenin could not attend himself. She helped him establish and grow the influence of what was called the Zimmerwald Left (the socialists not only opposed to the war but also strongly in favor of armed revolution and civil war). Against her wishes, Armand also capitulated to Lenin's insistence once again when he sent her on a rather dangerous mission to France (with a fake passport under an assumed name) to drum up French socialist support for the Zimmerwald Left in early 1916. When she didn't report in regularly enough, Lenin pelted her with messages, demanding more information. Given that France was at war, and that other prominent socialists were advocating contrary positions within the French left, Armand could only find support among youth groups and some syndicalist factions. Lenin questioned her level of effort, and this apparently infuriated her. During her final weeks in Paris, she ignored Lenin's messages and worked on her own projects. At the end of her trip, Armand bravely met with French soldiers and advocated desertion and revolution before she slipped back into Switzerland.

After April 1916, Armand distanced herself from Lenin, and pushed back against him in subtle and not so subtle ways. First, she chose to live on her own in various cities and towns around Switzerland, refusing to join Lenin and Krupskaya in Zurich where she would be subject to Lenin's constant demands. Angelica Balabanova once recalled that "[Armand] spoke a number of languages fluently, and in all of them repeated Lenin verbatim," but Armand's willingness to parrot him abruptly ceased.[21] She still did his translations into French and English, but she now refused to translate sentences that she disagreed with, which incensed Lenin. She also began challenging his ideas and pointing out instances where Lenin contradicted himself. In late 1916, he tried to convince her to go to Norway so she could be nearer to her children, hoping she would be willing to risk occasional visits to Russia to do his dirty work for him. Armand refused and stayed in Switzerland. He also tried to convince her to set up a Bolshevik publishing house (presumably with Alexander's money). Knowing Lenin as she did, Armand probably assumed that she would have to deal with all the logistics and translations while Lenin wrote all of the pamphlets. She rejected the idea. During 1916, Armand studied Marxist texts and clearly wanted to make some sort of intellectual contribution to the movement. She wanted to write her own articles, but Lenin continued to discourage her through his criticisms or make excuses for not publishing her work. Frustrated with him, she lived on her own until the moment she decided to return to Russia with Lenin, Krupskaya, and the other exiles in April 1917.

After the February revolution toppled the tsar and installed the provisional government, Armand could finally return to Russia without fear of persecution. Still deeply embroiled in World War I, the Provisional Government was losing popularity. Lenin, Krupskaya, Kollontai, Trotsky, and the other Bolsheviks began maneuvering to take control of the country. Because he trusted Armand, Lenin nominated her for various key positions within the party. She was the Moscow delegate to the Seventh All Party Conference (the so-called April conference) as one of only 151 delegates. But Armand also wanted to be with her children, whom she had not seen since their truncated holiday in 1914. Rather than subsuming herself in Bolshevik machinations in Petrograd, she spent the summer months of 1917 in the countryside caring for her youngest son, Andrei, who was ill once again. When unrest struck Petrograd during the turbulent July Days, Armand was out of the city and therefore avoided arrest. Her maternal duties similarly kept her out of the limelight during the October revolution, which finally put Lenin and the Bolsheviks in control.

Lenin immediately set about consolidating his power, and assigned Armand to undertake a wide variety of new responsibilities. Despite her previous frustrations with Lenin, Armand set to work as a faithful Bolshevik. By 1918, she was organizing conferences for working women, participating in the French section of the Russian Communist Party, teaching at party schools, and sitting on the All-Russian Central Executive Committee. She was also elected to the executive board of the Moscow Soviet and performed multiple administrative duties there. But Armand still harbored dreams of working to improve women's lives, and Lenin finally gave her the opportunity. The Bolsheviks desperately needed women's support as Russia withdrew from World War I and dealt with the immediate necessity of defeating the anti-Bolshevik White Army. Russia's wealthy elites fiercely resisted the nationalization of their properties and found allies among the Western nations fearful of Bolshevik-style revolutions in their own countries. Many peasants also supported the tsar and the church and turned against the Bolsheviks, creating chaos in the countryside.

During the civil war that began in 1918 and lingered through 1921, the new Bolshevik government relied on women to support the Red Army in auxiliary positions, and to replace men in the factories while they fought on the front lines. The education of peasant women, seen as repositories of tradition, conservatism, and reactionary support, became essential for the long-term survival of the new regime. The persistent resistance of the peasantry caused many problems for the Soviet state. At the same time, Lenin and the other Bolsheviks had to set aside their fears of feminism and the possibility of dividing the proletariat. They empowered Kollontai, Krupskaya, Armand and other women to push forward with their plans for women's emancipation. Patriarchal privilege was a small price to pay for the survival of the revolution if education and the socialization of domestic work would promote women's full incorporation into the labor force and increase their support for the Bolshevik cause. "If women's liberation is unthinkable without communism, then communism is unthinkable without women's liberation," said Inessa Armand.[22]

Whatever animosity developed between Lenin and Armand during the waning years of their exile in Western Europe faded after the October revolution. When Lenin's would-be assassin Fanny Kaplan shot him on August 30, 1918, Lenin asked for Armand; she spent days with Krupskaya at his bedside as he recovered. In return, Lenin gave Armand more responsibilities. In November 1918, Kollontai and Armand organized a massive national congress of working women. Expecting about 300 women to participate, Kollontai and Armand marveled when almost 1,200 women showed up from all over Russia, risking travel through a country torn apart by civil war. The logistics of housing and feeding all of these women (and sometimes their children) created chaos for the two Zhenotdel activists, who worked cordially together but were not nearly as close with each other as Armand and Krupskaya. The congress convened in the Hall of Unions, which thronged with delegates keen to discuss and debate the future of women in the new workers' state. Lenin and other major Bolshevik figures addressed the meeting, and Kollontai spoke about a future of new sexual relations without jealousy and selfishness. Armand stressed that bourgeois forms of domesticity held Soviet women back and emphasized the need for communal services to take over women's domestic duties. She would write in 1919: "Until the old forms of the family, domestic life, education and childrearing are abolished it is impossible to obliterate exploitation and enslavement, it is impossible to create the new person, impossible to build socialism."[23]

Soon after the national congress, Lenin dispatched Armand to France on an unsuccessful Red Cross mission, and she returned to Russia in August 1919 to head up the new Zhenotdel. Between 1919 and 1920, Armand dedicated herself entirely to improving the position of Soviet women, working long hours, eating poorly, smoking constantly, and generally failing to look after her health. And after Kollontai's heart attack in November of 1919, the Zhenotdel work fell almost entirely onto Armand's shoulders for four months. In addition to her advocacy for the expansion of public services for women, Armand organized meetings for women to discuss their problems and brainstorm solutions, as well as learn about new Soviet laws and how they affected their lives. Individual women were elected to represent their fellow workers or students at these "delegate meetings." By March 1920, Armand and the Zhenotdel managed to organize delegate meetings in all but two of the Soviet regions, a remarkable achievement in such a short period of time. Lenin obviously hoped that the meetings would win him women's support for his policies, but introducing women to the party's language and platform allowed them to press their own demands on the state. As historian Elizabeth Wood has argued, one reason Stalin later dismantled the Zhenotdel was because it grew too effective at representing women's needs.[24]

Also between 1919 and 1920, Armand finally began writing her own articles on women's issues for the women's pages of *Pravda* ("Truth"). She founded a journal specifically under the auspices of the Zhenotdel: *Kommunistika* ("The Woman Communist"), and she edited four full issues before her death. She also wrote a substantive pamphlet on "Workers in the International."[25] But perhaps the pinnacle of her career as a socialist women's activist came when she presided over the First International Conference of Communist Women held in July 1920.[26] In front of delegates from nineteen countries, Armand shared and advocated for the Soviet strategy of organizing women *within* party structures. This model of the top-down, state-backed, centralized women's organization prevailed in many states throughout the twentieth century.[27]

Organizing the delegate meetings as well as hosting the international conference and popularizing its resolutions pushed Armand to the brink of exhaustion. Seeing her pale, thin, and sick, Lenin suggested that she take a holiday in the Caucasus with her son Andrei. Utterly worn out, she agreed. But the civil war still raged in the south, and rumors of bandits circulated. Trying to micromanage Armand's life from Moscow, Lenin fretted for her safety and pestered her hosts to ensure her comfort. As bands of Reds and Whites skirmished in the mountains around her, Armand retreated inward. For all of her early passion and dedication, the forty-six-year-old found herself depleted by the tasks of building the new world of which she had so long dreamed. In his biography of Armand,

Michael Pearson quotes at length from the passages she wrote in her final weeks of life (in which she refers to Lenin as "V.I."):

> I also feel a wild desire to be alone. I am tired even when other people are talking around me, let alone having to speak myself. I wonder if this feeling of inner death will ever pass. I have reached a point where I find it strange when other people laugh and have such pleasure in talking ... Now I don't like people so much. Previously I approached everyone with a warm feeling. Now I am indifferent to everyone and bored by them all. The only warm feelings I have left are for the children and V.I. In all other respects it's as if my heart has died; as if, having given up all of my strength, all my passion to V.I. and the work, I have exhausted all sources of love and compassion toward people to whom previously I was so richly open. I have no relations with other people, except in my work. And people

Inessa Armand in 1920

feel this deadness in me and they pay me back with the same indifference and antipathy. And now even my attitude toward my work is fading.[28]

In this state of mind, feeling helpless and depressed, Inessa Armand died of cholera on September 24, 1920. According to witnesses who met her body at the train station, Lenin was so devastated by her death he could not speak. In October 1920, Inessa Armand lay in state in the very Hall of Unions where she had presided over the First International Conference of Communist Women just a few months before. A procession of thousands, singing "The Internationale," followed her body as it was borne through Moscow from the Hall of Unions to Red Square. In 1963, the scholar Bertram Wolfe spoke with the Bolshevik Angelica Balabanova about Armand's funeral; Lenin had apparently pleaded with Balabanova to give a speech, but she was unprepared and hesitant. She told Wolfe:

> Fortunately, at the last moment Kollontai arrived, and delivered a moving address. I cast sidelong glances at Lenin. He was plunged in despair, his cap down over his eyes; small as he was, he seemed to shrink and grow smaller. He looked pitiful and broken in spirit. I never saw him look like that before. It was something more than the loss of a "good Bolshevik" or a good friend. He had lost some one very dear and very close to him and made no effort to conceal it.[29]

Armand's remains are buried in the Kremlin Wall Necropolis, where she shares a memorial stone with the American journalist John Reed who died just two months after her. In her own memoirs, Emma Goldman reports being deeply moved by the speech Alexandra Kollontai gave over the grave of John Reed, but Kollontai must have also had Armand in mind when she spoke these words: "We call ourselves Communists, but are we really that? Do we not rather draw the life essence from those who come to us, and when they are no longer of use, we let them fall by the wayside, neglected and forgotten? Our Communism and our comradeship are dead letters if we do not give out of ourselves to those who need us. Let us beware of such Communism. It slays the best in our ranks."[30]

Inessa Armand was certainly among the best in their ranks.

5

The International Amazon

Elena Lagadinova (1930–2017)

Ten years after Inessa Armand's untimely death, a child was born across the Black Sea in Bulgaria, the country whose first post-independence constitution had been prepared by Alexandra Kollontai's father. In 1941, while Lyudmila Pavlichenko picked off fascists one by one on the Eastern Front, this child, now eleven years old, risked her life to run food and messages to the guerilla fighters hiding in the Pirin mountains around the small town of Razlog. Elena Lagadinova was the youngest girl partisan struggling against the Nazi-allied Bulgarian monarchy during World War II, earning herself the nickname "the Amazon." Unlike Pavlichenko, who fired a rifle, Lagadinova had only a small pistol that she wore on a chain around her neck to avoid misplacing it. And while Pavlichenko died when I was four years old, I had the honor of first meeting Elena Lagadinova when I was forty.

In the summer of 2010, I began searching for members of the official Bulgarian delegation who had attended the First United Nations International Women's Year Conference in Mexico City in 1975. Lagadinova led that delegation, and I was delighted to learn that she was still alive and living in Sofia. Lagadinova had also lived in Moscow while Kollontai and Pavlichenko were still alive, although they never met. As she studied for her PhD in plant genetics in the early 1950s, Lagadinova benefitted from the very programs that Kollontai, Krupskaya, and Armand had a hand in creating.

Elena Lagadinova in 1944

Unfortunately, Lagadinova refused to meet with me. She guarded her privacy and feared the censorious political climate of post-socialist Bulgaria where younger people derided women of her age and pedigree as pathetic "red grandmothers." Lagadinova had endured many accusations and betrayals after 1989. At the age of eighty, she harbored little hope that an American scholar would listen to her story without prejudice in 2010. Only the strategic intervention of my ex-father-in-law, a former colleague of hers, finally swayed her. In many ways, Lagadinova became for me a living link to the long heritage of socialist women stretching back to Kollontai, Krupskaya, Armand, and Pavlichenko.

A true red diaper baby, Lagadinova was born into a poor family of committed socialist revolutionaries. Her father was Atanas Lagadinov, a peddler, a carriage driver, and a veteran of the Balkan Wars. Atanas traveled around his country and

witnessed the growing prosperity of Bulgaria's small bourgeois class, compared to the desperate poverty of the peasants.
His experience of war had taught him that peasant lives were
expendable—little more than cannon fodder—and that only
a revolution would improve their living standards. Atanas
founded the Razlog Branch of the Bulgarian Communist Party
in the year following the Bolshevik revolution, and he participated in what is often referred to by Bulgarians as the world's
"first anti-fascist uprising" in 1923. His wife, Fidanka Lagadinova, had died when young Elena Lagadinova was only
four years old in 1934, leaving Lagadinova to be raised by
Atanas and her older brothers. She was barely old enough to
remember when her eldest brother fled into exile in the Soviet
Union because of his underground work with the communists.

Bulgaria had been liberated from five centuries of Ottoman
domination in 1878, but its largely peasant economy lagged

Elena Lagadinova at her mother's funeral in 1934

far behind those of Western Europe, and the young nation eagerly imported socialist and communist ideas from both Germany and Russia. The historian Maria Todorova has uncovered many early Bulgarian translations of the works of Marx, Engels, August Bebel, and other socialist theorists and revealed the widespread enthusiasm for communist ideals among Bulgaria's literate and educated classes.[1] Each of Atanas's three sons embraced the revolutionary spirit of the time, bringing their family much persecution and sorrow over the years leading up to World War II when Bulgaria signed the Tripartite Pact on March 1, 1941.

By the spring of 1944, Bulgarian forces occupied large portions of Northern Greece and Eastern Yugoslavia as the Red Army marched west. After the German defeat at Stalingrad, inspired partisan bands increased their attacks against Nazi supply lines and sabotaged local factories. The British Royal Air Force began dropping provisions and armaments as the ranks of the guerillas swelled, and the government of King Boris III deployed the gendarmerie to try to subdue the partisan threat. The gendarmes torched the homes of suspected partisan families, and anyone caught aiding the guerillas could be arrested, tortured, and shot. Hoping to enlist the cooperation of the peasants, the Bulgarian minister of the interior promised large bounties for each severed partisan head brought into the authorities.

On May 31, 1944, the gendarmes threw incendiary bombs into Lagadinova's house, barely giving her enough time to escape. "I never knew shoes until I was eleven years old," she explained to me, "and when they burned my house down, I cried because they burned my only pair of shoes." Barefoot, she fled to find her father and brothers, terrified of what the soldiers might do to her if they caught her before she reached the safety of the mountains. She spent the summer of 1944 hiding and fighting until early September, when the Red Army neared Bulgaria and the local communists rose up and overthrew the government, switching sides to join the Allied forces and paving the way for the establishment of the People's Republic of Bulgaria. Although Lagadinova lost her second eldest brother, Assen (who had been decapitated for the bounty), the rest of the Lagadinov family survived and descended from the mountains as heroes of the war. Little Lagadinova rode victoriously into town on a great white steed, and she became something of a folk hero and anti-fascist role model. As with Pavlichenko in the Soviet Union, journalists and propagandists celebrated Lagadinova's participation in the war. From Sofia to Moscow, children's magazines featured her portrait, told her story, and encouraged socialist boys and girls to "be brave like the Amazon."

After World War II, Lagadinova married a fellow partisan from her brigade and moved to the Soviet Union, where she pursued her doctoral degree in agrobiology at the prestigious Moscow Timiryazev Agricultural Academy between 1948 and 1953. She had two children in the USSR and, after earning her degree, completed two research internships in Sweden and the

Elena Lagadinova with friends in 1948 in the USSR

United Kingdom where she learned some English in addition to her fluent Russian. When she returned to Sofia, she was given a research associate position at the Plant Breeding Institute within the Bulgarian Academy of Sciences. Genetically selected seeds, combined with the introduction of mechanized and collectivized agriculture, allowed the new socialist government to subsidize wheat. Having grown up eating rough cornmeal mixed with water, Lagadinova rejoiced at her part in making bread available to even her poorest compatriots. In 1959, the government of Bulgaria awarded Lagadinova the prestigious Order of Cyril and Methodius, in recognition of her scientific achievements in the successful breeding of a hybrid of wheat and rye.

Over the years that I met with her, Lagadinova unearthed many folders of documents and photographs from her life. A consummate archivist, she organized her papers by eras. I found copies of some of her most important papers in English from her scientific work between 1953 and 1967, such as "Triticale, a Valuable Starting Material in Hybridization with Common Winter Wheat Triticum Aestivum" (1962) in the *Journal of the Agricultural Research Institute of the Hungarian Academy of Sciences* and "Study on the Character of Inheriting the Qualitative Elements in the First Generation Intervariety Hybridization of Winter Wheat" (1963) in the *Comptes Rendus de l'Académie bulgare de Sciences*. Lagadinova radiated pride when she showed me these articles. Although the scientific language eluded me, I could see that she still loved science and might have regretted trading in her lab for a career in politics.

That professional transition started with a letter that she penned to the then Soviet premier Leonid Brezhnev in May of 1967, complaining about the ways that socialist countries organized and disseminated their scientific research. After World War II, Bulgaria lacked specialists in many fields, including science and engineering. Backward peasant countries with little industrial capacity prior to the advent of communism—such as Russia in 1917 or Bulgaria, Romania, and Yugoslavia in 1945—had not passed through the historical stage of capitalism necessary to industrialize their economies. The few specialists that existed before 1945 often fled to the West or, if they stayed, were members of the former bourgeois class and therefore hostile to the politics of the centralized economy. But postwar Bulgaria needed these specialists, which meant working together with experts trained under the previous regime. To solve the problem of politically unreliable specialists in state-owned enterprises (and, presumably, to prevent sabotage), loyal party members were assigned to watch over the work of the experts.

Unfortunately, many of these party members lacked the relevant education or a basic understanding of technical matters. They often caused trouble by increasing bureaucracy or otherwise stifling innovation in the name of abstract Marxist principles. Scientific knowledge also became politicized and highly qualified scientists could fall afoul of the regime for trivial opinions. Lagadinova was among the first postwar generation of scientists trained in the Soviet Union who were also committed to the ideals of socialism, and she thought that the Communist Party's babysitters were no longer necessary. Almost all socialist countries faced this tension between lionizing the members of the working class and relying on a cadre of well-trained experts; Lagadinova therefore believed that Brezhnev alone, as the leader of the communist world, could resolve the conflicts she faced in her daily life.

Lagadinova took a huge risk by sending such a letter to the Soviet Union, which could easily have cost her the research associate position at the Bulgarian Academy of Sciences. The Bulgarian authorities intercepted the letter; luckily for Lagadinova, however, Bulgaria's leader, Todor Zhivkov, agreed that his country's economic progress was being hampered by too many layers of bureaucracy and outdated paranoia about bourgeois spies and saboteurs. Zhivkov was a former partisan who had risen to power in 1954 after Stalin's death. Contrary to Western stereotypes of East European communist leaders as brutal dictators, many committed reformers within the ranks of the communist parties such as Zhivkov believed in the ideals of socialism and hoped to improve the system from inside of it; these included Josip Broz Tito in Yugoslavia, Nikita Khrushchev in the USSR, Alexander Dubček in Czechoslovakia, and, perhaps most consequentially, Mikhail Gorbachev, the last Soviet premier. After Khrushchev's infamous secret speech in 1956, Zhivkov hoped to replicate the Khrushchev Thaw in his own country, liberalizing the communist system both politically and economically. Lagadinova's letter to Brezhnev suddenly put her on Zhivkov's radar as a principled communist willing to stand up for her beliefs in the name of improving the system. Zhivkov also knew that Lagadinova came from a renowned family of partisans and, although she had been working quietly in a research lab for thirteen years, most Bulgarians still remembered her as the Amazon: the brave young girl with the pistol attached to a chain around her neck.

"One day, they sent a car for me while I was at the Academy," Lagadinova told me in 2011. "I was in my lab coat, in the middle of an experiment. I told them to wait but they told me to come immediately. I thought I was being arrested. Instead, I learned that they wanted to make me a secretary of the Fatherland Front and a new president of the Women's Committee."

Zhivkov had a serious problem that he needed Elena Lagadinova to help him solve. After 1945, Bulgaria's new communist constitution guaranteed full equality to women. The state had forged ahead with plans for women's emancipation, following a path more or less the same as the one Kollontai, Krupskaya, and Armand had developed in the early years of the Soviet Union. Male labor shortages precipitated the need to mobilize women into the formal workforce to help rapidly modernize Bulgaria's largely agricultural economy. The new state invested in women's education and training as hundreds of thousands of peasants left the villages and poured into Bulgaria's new towns and cities. In just two decades between 1945 and 1965, life expectancy rose, infant and maternal mortality rates fell, and Bulgarians enjoyed living standards that they could have scarcely imagined before the war. But the increasing independence of women combined with rapid urbanization led to plummeting birth rates as Bulgaria experienced a sudden demographic transition from high to low fertility.

Across the socialist bloc (and in some Western countries as well), increases in professional opportunities for women suppressed birth rates, and leaders such as Todor Zhivkov worried about the long-term economic impacts of a shrinking population and labor force. The availability of abortion more or less on demand exacerbated this problem; nearby Romania had suspended all reproductive rights for women in 1966 to increase the birth rate. Bulgaria's leaders were considering a similar proposal but feared that outlawing abortion would only push the practice underground and run the risk of antagonizing the women whose support they needed to further grow the economy. Prior to 1968, the Women's Committee worked internationally and concern for Bulgaria's women workers and mothers was largely divided among other social organizations: the trade unions, cooperative associations, and youth organizations. A reorganization of the committee to increase its domestic responsibilities would allow for the development and implementation of local solutions to the demographic crisis. Zhivkov considered this a scientific problem, and therefore wanted a scientist to lead the efforts to find its solution. He chose Lagadinova to lead a Bulgarian women's revolution.

For her part, Lagadinova preferred to stay in her lab with her seeds, but ever the good communist, she accepted the responsibility that had fallen on her shoulders. Pregnant with her third child, she was elected the president of the Women's Committee and busied herself with her new work. Adamantly opposed to an outright ban on abortion, Lagadinova did something only rarely attempted by communist leaders up to that point: she asked women about their problems. In 1969, Lagadinova and the editorial collective of the state women's magazine, together with the National Statistical Institute, conducted a sociological survey of over 16,000 respondents. The questionnaire asked women about their daily lives, the challenges they faced, and their hopes for the future. The survey revealed that most Bulgarian women wanted more children but struggled to balance their responsibilities as both workers and mothers. Between their labor obligations and domestic responsibilities, Lagadinova discovered that women worked what they called a "second shift"[2] which left them little leisure time and forced them to limit the size of their families. Husbands rarely helped out around the house, and the state had yet to commit the resources necessary to socialize most of the unpaid labor women did in the home. Bulgarian women felt exhausted.

In many Western nations today, debates about work/family balance continue to rage, and the coronavirus pandemic revealed just how little progress has been made in this area. As childcare centers and schools closed down, it was primarily women who withdrew from the labor force to handle all of the caregiving and homeschooling required. But the state socialist countries in Eastern Europe were debating these issues as early as the 1920s in the Soviet Union and throughout the 1960s in Bulgaria and elsewhere. Betty Friedan published *The Feminine Mystique* in 1963, and white, middle-class American women were taking their first tentative steps into the labor force when public discussions about the need for universal childcare exploded in the Eastern Bloc. As the mother of three children, Lagadinova personally understood the challenges faced by working women, and she tirelessly pressured the country's leaders in the Politburo (all but one of whom were male) to expend the resources necessary to lighten women's burdens.

Lagadinova and her colleagues could point to the texts of Engels, Bebel, and Lenin; the practical experiments of women like Kollontai, Krupskaya, and Armand; and the courage and dedication of fighters like Pavlichenko to demand that the men in their party live up to the socialist promise of true emancipation for women and ensure public provision of services to support mothers and children. They devised a concrete set of policies combining child allowances and generous job-protected maternity leave for all women workers, including those in agriculture. Time on leave would officially count as labor service for the calculation of pensions, and women could later choose to share these leaves with fathers or grandparents. As with other states in the socialist bloc, the Bulgarians promised to build a wide network of new nurseries and kindergartens so that every child had a place in one if needed. Their proposals drained many resources from the state budget and Lagadinova in particular met constant resistance from her own party comrades, who considered women's issues less important than the other urgent tasks facing the Bulgarian economy.

As in the early days of the Soviet Union, the foundations of patriarchy remained largely unshaken despite women's contributions to the socialist project, and sexism persisted in both the workplace and the home. Lagadinova herself admitted to me that she had often struggled with the need to make time for her children since both she and her husband served in high-ranking political positions in the Bulgarian government. By all accounts, Lagadinova was what Americans would call a "workaholic." She shared with Kollontai a "flaming intensity" that allowed her to get things done, but she was more like

Armand in her often-frustrated attempts to tend to the needs of her family. Traditional Bulgarian expectations of motherhood and of women's proper roles dogged her career at every turn, and she fumed against what she called the "wooden headed" mentality of her male compatriots.

This did not prevent Lagadinova from challenging her male comrades in positions of authority. In addition to my many interviews with Lagadinova and access to her personal archives, I spent a decade working with the documentary records of the Bulgarian Women's Committee in the Central State Archives. Folder after folder of evidence revealed how fiercely Lagadinova and her colleagues had advocated for women behind the scenes, navigating a bureaucratic and economically constipated system.

As with all planned economies, consumer shortages plagued the Bulgarian population, and the goods produced often reflected the priorities of male planners with little interest in the needs of women. A 1977 letter that Lagadinova addressed to the Ministry of Trade and Services critiqued the lack of quality and availability of women's clothing: "Jersey dresses, which are very practical, are rarely available in the stores. When they are, there are only limited sizes and they are not in the most fashionable styles."[3] She went on to point out that the central planners did a good job of making men's underwear, but undergarments for women and children were generally scarce and "not in all the sizes or patterns or colors that the population is seeking."[4] Then she wrote to the Central Committee of the Communist Party and complained that "the clothes which can be found now in the stores for our citizens are the ugliest that can be seen."[5]

Lagadinova and the Women's Committee also researched the layout of Western self-serve supermarkets as they tried to streamline and improve the shopping experience under a socialist economy.[6] Because of constant shortages, socialist foodstuffs and other goods were often kept behind a counter and distributed by a salesperson to ensure that no single customer bought more than necessary for one family. But the slowness of the salespeople contributed to the long lines that we still associate with socialist countries today.[7] The Women's Committee argued that the long queues for basic foodstuffs created an extra burden on women in the family, and that Western-style self-service supermarkets would be more efficient. Unfortunately, the self-service model often led to hoarding as shoppers overbought in hopes that they could later barter the goods with their colleagues, neighbors, and relatives. These hoarding behaviors often led to empty shelves.

Like Kollontai, Krupskaya, and Armand before her, Lagadinova also emphasized the need for more nurseries and preschools, hoping to lessen the burdens associated with raising children by publicly providing high quality childcare. But the rapidly industrializing Bulgarian economy lacked the resources to build and staff these institutions. As in the early Soviet Union, male leaders understood that it was more cost-effective to have women provide childcare for free in the home as one of their "natural" maternal duties. In 1987, Lagadinova spoke about the importance of persistence, recounting

Elena Lagadinova on her fiftieth birthday with comrades

the problems that the Women's Committee had experienced in dealing with the recalcitrance of men around the issue of childcare:

> The Committee of Women has the idea that more money should be spent for the construction of kindergartens as 80 per cent of children are in kindergartens but we think that 100 per cent of them should be in kindergartens and more should be built. During the discussion they said, "Elena, we have no money for kindergartens." Then I start writing letters to the higher institutions to prove that this is an objective necessity. If we succeed in convincing them by the Parliament session; okay; if we don't succeed, we'll continue the discussion during the [next] Parliament session. But my experience shows that new things find their way with difficulty, and to succeed, you should be convinced, you should know how to convince people, and you have to have arguments.[8]

The Women's Committee surveys revealed that working women spent their "second shifts" cooking and cleaning up after meals, in addition to shopping and taking care of children. In a 1977 interview, Lagadinova explained that the committee was putting pressure on schools and enterprises to expand public catering to help tackle the problems "concerning the actual equality of women." As in the early Soviet Union, social-ist states subsidized meals eaten at school, at the workplace, and in neighborhood restaurants like the famous milk bars in Poland.[9] Access to ready-made meals for all workers and students would reduce the housework required of working women. Lagadinova explained that while 40 percent of Bul-garia's students in first through eighth grade ate their breakfast and lunch at schools, the committee hoped to dramatically increase this percentage in order to "shorten to [a] minimum the time women use to cook."[10] She also hoped that the can-teens in workplaces would be able to prepare meals (or their components) for women to take home with them at the end of the day, cutting down the time associated with shopping and cooking. In one of my interviews with her, Lagadinova told me that she was famous for taking her lunches in the canteens and cafeterias when she visited schools and enterprises around the country to check the quality of the subsidized food. Lagadinova understood that public catering would only work if the food tasted good; otherwise children and husbands would continue to clamor for home-cooked meals.

The Women's Committee also proposed that elementary and middle school students should have after-school clubs and activities. Furthermore, taking into account that the burden of homework supervision usually fell on mothers, they advised that all students should complete their homework at school so that "when they go back home they will be free from school obligations and will have more time to spend with their working parents."[11] Different levels of parental involvement in homework also exacerbated educational inequalities across families, and homework clubs could provide valuable support to students in need of extra guidance. Lagadinova and her comrades promoted concrete policy changes to incrementally reduce the hours working mothers spent on their second shifts while also trying to ensure that all children enjoyed the nutrition and educational opportunities they needed to thrive.

Following five years of tireless effort, the ideas and proposals of the Committee of the Bulgarian Women's Movement finally found success. Based on the surveys they conducted among Bulgarian women, the Committee's policy recommendations were codified in a special 1973 Politburo decision: "Enhancing the Role of Women in the Building of a Developed Socialist Society." This decision authorized massive budget expenditures to expand state supports for women and families.[12] In addition, it called for the re-education of boys and men to challenge gender stereotypes about "women's work."

The reduction and alleviation of woman's household work depends greatly on the common participation of the two spouses in the organization of family life. It is therefore imperative a) to combat outdated views, habits, and attitudes as regards the allocation of work within the family; b) to prepare young men for the performance of household duties from childhood and adolescence both by the school and society and by the family.[13]

While it is true that this Politburo decision used explicitly pro-natalist language, the document emerged from a "bottom-up" intervention in the workings of the socialist state, something that Western observers have considered impossible in a so-called totalitarian society. The surveys of Bulgarian women revealed that most wanted to both work outside the home and have children, but they needed more help in finding a sane balance between the two endeavors, which is what the Bulgarian state gave them. By the time that Elena Lagadinova led the official Bulgarian delegation to the United Nations First World Conference of Women in 1975, her small Balkan country had one of the most progressive social systems in place for working women compared not only to the capitalist countries in the West and the Global South but to other socialist countries as well.[14]

During the UN Decade for Women (1976–85), Lagadinova circumvented the globe forging relationships with over a hundred women's organizations (even though this extensive travel separated her from her family back at home). The Women's Committee's success on the international stage translated into greater power at home, and Lagadinova used the Committee's growing international clout to advocate for changes in the Bulgarian Family and Labor Codes. Although she was part of the communist establishment—Lagadinova would eventually become a member of both parliament and the Central Committee of the Bulgarian Communist Party—she made many enemies by holding Bulgarian leaders accountable within the framework of their own laws and the international conventions they had signed. The Women's Committee also antagonized the male directors of Bulgarian enterprises who refused to grant pregnant women their legal rights, and relentlessly badgered state planners to provide the services that families needed. In 1975, for instance, Elena Lagadinova wrote a "warning note" to the vice president of the Council of Ministers and the president of the Commission on Living Conditions complaining that a certain factory in the town of Mihailovgrad did not yet have a workers' cafeteria. This meant that the 830 women workers (out of 1,007 workers in total) ate meals they had brought from home at their workstations. The Committee insisted that a cafeteria be built immediately to give the workers a place to socialize and rest, and to save the women the time it took to make their lunches.[15] This constant attention to the increased socialization of domestic work characterized all twenty-two years of Lagadinova's leadership, and as her influence grew, so too did the internal surveillance of her actions. She knew the secret police had bugged her home and that every speech she made was scrutinized for any hint of betrayal to the wider cause of Bulgarian socialism. Lagadinova once explained to me that she could measure how much change she was affecting by the growing level of interest of Bulgaria's secret police.

Lagadinova was active not only in Bulgaria, but also made efforts to bridge the worlds of women divided by geopolitics. After the United Nations Conference in 1975 she began to build a wide-ranging international network with women in what were then called "developing countries," providing both material and logistical support for new women's committees and movements in Africa, Asia, and Latin America. She even reached out across the Iron Curtain, joining forces with Western women advocating for peace and disarmament in the 1980s. Jean Lipman-Blumen, an American professor who

Elena Lagadinova with a
Congolese comrade in 1981

wrote a book on "connective leadership," lauded Lagadinova's natural talent for working with others:

> I first met Elena Lagadinova in Sofia in 1980, at a conference
> cosponsored by the U.S. National Science Foundation. The
> Cold War was still icy, but Lagadinova showed little patience
> for political impediments to collaboration. With pragmatic
> enthusiasm, she assured the conferees, "Do not worry about
> ideology and government barriers. The work we have to do for
> women in both of our countries is too important for that. We
> shall manage together!" The skeptical American visitors, ini-
> tially on guard against communist manipulation, soon learned
> her word was as true as her vision. The second time I met
> Lagadinova was in 1985, during the United Nations Confer-
> ence of the Status of Women, in Nairobi. There, the conference
> delegates elected Lagadinova rapporteur, testimony to how
> much she was esteemed by an immense international network
> of policy makers, political activists, and academics.[16]

Lagadinova's global influence reached its apex in Nairobi when she became the face of the international women's movement to the global press. A quarter of a century after the event, Elena Lagadinova confirmed that her election as general rapporteur was one of the highlights of her long career. She told me how she deliberately used her position to draw the world's attention to the achievements of women living in socialist societies. At her first major press conference, Lagadinova recalled doing her best both to endear herself to the world's journalists and to dispel what she called "anti-socialist propaganda." When she took the podium, her pulse racing, she decided to address the assembled reporters in English, although she usually spoke in Russian at UN meetings. Lagadinova explained to me that Western women often harbored negative stereotypes about socialist women, and she wanted everyone to know that she was a mother as well as a politician. "I now shall try to speak in English," she told the assembled reporters. "And if my daughter, who is the third (and they all speak English very well) would be hearing now how I speak in English, she would say, 'Oy Mama! Mama! What kind of courage you have! All these two hundred people, to speak to in a language you don't know!'"[17] Everyone in the room laughed. Although Lagadinova gave the rest of her report in Russian, she thought that her brief foray into English had made her more relatable to the Western and Kenyan journalists covering the conference.

Lagadinova also mobilized her networks to meet influential journalists and disseminate information about her country, distributing thousands of brochures and pamphlets about Bulgaria's public services for women and families in English, Spanish, French, German, and Arabic. Lagadinova told me that representatives of the other socialist countries marveled at the number of articles written about Bulgaria, which she claimed exceeded the number of articles written about all of the other socialist countries combined (including the USSR).

Lagadinova said she knew how to work with different types of people. "You have to make contact with people with the heart. Not with the mind. The mind is ideology," she explained to me over tea one day. "Human contact is something that everyone understands even if they have different ideology."

In 1986, Lagadinova became a member of the board of trustees of the United Nations Institute for Training Women (INSTRAW), where she served for two years and continued to champion women's issues on the global stage. She traveled around the world sharing Bulgaria's experiences with socialist and non-socialist nations alike, including China, Korea, Cambodia, Yemen, Ethiopia, Nicaragua, Greece, and Turkey. In 1987, Amina Bose, a journalist for *Roshni: The Journal of the All India Women's Conference*, interviewed the visiting Bulgarian, and reported that she was impressed by Lagadinova's "optimism ... her sense of humor, her faith in human beings and her concern for human dignity."[18] Lagadinova showed me letters from politicians, peace activists, scientists, and feminists from across the world that she had saved in her personal archives, all thanking her for some thoughtful gift or act of kindness. By November 1989, when East European state socialism finally imploded, Elena Lagadinova counted among the most well-known Bulgarian politicians outside her country.

Before the disintegration of the Soviet Union in 1991, the Claremont Graduate School in California awarded Lagadinova their President's Medal of Outstanding Achievement. The honorary citation read:

> The world, Elena Lagadinova, is your deliberately chosen arena. Dedicated resistance fighter, recognized scientist, and stateswoman acclaimed by the international community of nations, your contributions make a trajectory that inspires and astounds us. Dedicated to improving the position of women in all countries around the globe, you have the wisdom to

conceptualize women's issues not as theirs alone, but as societies [*sic*] most fundamental challenges ... Long before a new world order emerged, you envisioned one. You acted as if it already existed, and through your actions you contributed to its emergence. You reached beyond the narrow confines of party and nationality to create an international network of scholars and policymakers devoted to the improvement of women's lives. Through your work with the United Nations, you have influenced women's lives throughout the world, and through them the destinies of their families.[19]

The end of state socialism in Eastern Europe came suddenly and almost without warning. In a 1987 interview, Lagadinova explained: "I think that until the moment I stop breathing, I will be actively involved in the political activity of my country. We have a variety of activities for retired people to be included actively in social life, and as long as I have the strength I will

Elena Lagadinova in Nigeria in 1988

try to be useful to society."[20] But, in 1990, at the age of sixty, Lagadinova found herself forced into retirement, pushed out of power, and soon forgotten as a relic of an unseemly past as Bulgaria dove headfirst into globalized capitalism. When I met her in 2010, she was spending long days on her own in a cold apartment because her small pension barely covered the costs of central heating. Her work for Bulgarian women and her contributions to the global women's movement had been forgotten, but she never stopped believing that another world was possible.

Yes, the socialism that she had fought for had failed, but this did not mean that others could not learn from her experiences and those of the members of the Women's Committee. The moral vacuum that followed the collapse of socialism in Bulgaria—the rise of the mafia, the crime and corruption, the poverty and unemployment, the conspiracy theories, the massive out-migration of young people and the collapsing birth rate—proved to Lagadinova that her socialism, for all of its many faults, had at least raised living standards and promised some form of security and stability in ordinary working people's lives. She was the first to admit the many problems with the old system: the travel restrictions, the secret police, the consumer shortages, the ugly clothes, and lack of political freedoms. But, like many other socialist idealists before her, Lagadinova believed that the old system could have been reformed from within rather than completely dismantled.

Over our long conversations during my visits to Bulgaria, Lagadinova and I discussed everything from politics to religion to practical ways to fund universal childcare and the importance of social dreaming in the face of widespread despair and apathy. In 2015, I published a book that partially focused on Lagadinova's experiences as a partisan.[21] By coincidence, Jerry Brown, then governor of the state of California, stumbled upon a copy of this book in the City Lights bookstore in San Francisco and contacted me to help arrange a

Elena Lagadinova and Governor Jerry Brown of California in June 2016

meeting for him with Lagadinova in Bulgaria. In the summer of 2016, Governor Brown and his wife flew to Sofia to have tea in Lagadinova's apartment. She reveled in the attention and did her best to convince Brown that politicians had a duty to provide social services to support working people. "She was so energetic," Brown later told me. "Her English wasn't so good, but I could feel her passion and vitality."

I last met Lagadinova in May of 2017 when I briefly visited Bulgaria: an in-and-out trip to the archives to put the finishing touches on an article I was writing. We sat for a few hours in her dining room, chatting and commiserating over the rise of right-wing parties in Eastern Europe, the increasing influence of the Alternative for Germany (AfD) Party, and the unexpected election of Donald Trump. I despaired for the future, suggesting that I might emigrate to New Zealand. Before I left that evening, she told me: "Don't run. Fight. And remember, it is not enough to struggle against the things you hate. You have to stand up for something you believe in."

Elena Lagadinova died in her sleep just five months later at the age of eighty six. When I received the email from her daughter about her death, I recalled her last words to me.

Lagadinova will never see the more perfect world she tried to build, but it consoles me to think that she passed from this world still dreaming of it. I like to imagine her in the afterlife, pistol on a chain around her neck, young again, and ready to fight.

Conclusion

Nine Lessons We Can Learn
from the Red Valkyries

Between 1869, when Nadezhda Krupskaya was born, and 2017, when Elena Lagadinova died, the world for ordinary women in Eastern Europe drastically changed, and largely for the better. No, things are not (and never were) perfect; there has been resistance and regression. And yes, there remains much work to be done. Many challenges still lie ahead. But the women profiled within these pages oversaw more than a century of profound changes in the status of women in their countries, changes that reverberated across the world— not only in the countries that followed the socialist path to national liberation and economic development during the Cold War, but also the Western capitalist countries that considered socialism an existential threat. Because of the Eastern Bloc's attention to workers' rights, women's rights, and civil rights, Western governments have often been forced to respond to accusations that the West's commitments to democracy only extend to protecting the freedoms of wealthy white (or ethnic majority) men. By highlighting the contradictions of capitalism, international accusations from the socialist countries helped to create essential cracks that domestic social movements rushed in to exploit. Popular anger and outrage from the so-called grass roots mixed with international pressure to force progressive social change around the globe.[1]

This international pressure succeeded because state socialist societies, for all of socialism's faults and shortcomings,
actually improved the lives of millions of men and women
throughout the twentieth century. Some basic statistics illus-
trate this point: Although Russia started out with significantly
lower life expectancies than those found in the West, it rapidly
closed the gap during the state socialist era. In 1910, life
expectancy at birth in tsarist Russia was thirty-three years,
compared to fifty-three in the UK and fifty-two in the United
States.[2] By 1970, life expectancy in the Soviet Union more
than doubled to sixty-eight years, compared to seventy-two
in the UK and seventy in the United States. Despite the many
troubles with central planning, the massive human costs of
the collectivization of agriculture, and the brutal decades of
Stalinist rule, on the most basic level, Soviet citizens lived
longer and healthier lives than Russians had under the tsar.
While they started out far below their Western counterparts
in terms of economic development, the Soviets reduced the life
expectancy gap with the Americans to only two years under
the socialist system. This is not an endorsement of Stalin or
of Soviet authoritarianism. It is merely a recognition that the
entire history of the Soviet Union (and of socialism, for that
matter) cannot be reduced to the horrific crimes of Stalinism.

These same gains in life expectancy also occurred in the
East European countries that embraced socialism after 1945.
Life expectancies in Czechoslovakia, Hungary, and Poland
had been closer than Russia's to those of Western Europe,
and rapidly closed the gap after socialism was implemented.
Less developed countries such as Romania, Bulgaria, Albania,
and Yugoslavia, however, started the twentieth century with
average life expectancies far below those of the United States
and the United Kingdom, but experienced rapid increases
in life expectancy with the spread of universal healthcare
systems. Average Bulgarian life expectancy was fifty-two years
in 1945 when the country became part of the Eastern Bloc

and began building a socialist economy. By 1990, after forty-five years of communism, life expectancy had increased to seventy-one years.[3] In Albania, average life expectancy in 1945 was forty years. After the 1946 establishment of the People's Republic of Albania, life expectancy steadily climbed to seventy-two years by 1990, a massive gain of thirty-two years in just over four decades.[4]

More support and prenatal care for mothers also meant that infant mortality rates fell during the state socialist period. In 1915, mortality for Russian children under the age of one was 267 per 1,000 children; by 1990, just before the socialist system collapsed, the rate was only 24 per 1,000.[5] Bulgarian infant mortality rates also fell from 130 per 1,000 children in 1945 to 14 per 1,000 in 1990.[6] Literacy rates for the population, and especially for women, also expanded dramatically after 1917. In 1897, the percentage of Russians over the age of nine who could read stood at 35 percent of men and only 12.5 percent of women in the rural areas, and 66 percent of men and 46 percent of women in the urban areas.[7] By 1920, only three years after the revolution, rural male literacy rates grew to 52 percent and rural female literacy doubled to 25 percent. In the urban areas, 81 percent of men and 67 percent of women could read by 1920. Literacy rates for the population, both rural and urban, continued to grow until 1959 when the Soviet Union achieved almost universal literacy. Similar achievements could be found across the socialist world, particularly among women. The vast majority of Albanian women could not read before 1945, but the country achieved almost universal literacy for people under forty only ten years later.[8]

The Soviets and other state socialist governments also rapidly expanded educational opportunities, including for the youngest children, precisely as envisioned by Kollontai, Krupskaya, and Armand. In *Small Comrades: Revolutionizing Childhood in Soviet Russia, 1917–1932*, the historian Lisa A.

Kirschenbaum details the early challenges faced by the Commissariat of Enlightenment, including the chaotic conditions of the civil war and the famine that followed. Kirschenbaum reveals how local Soviet administrations, despite many constraints, followed through on plans to provide preschools for all children. In 1918, the Moscow province set up twenty-three kindergartens, eight nurseries, and thirteen summer playgrounds, but by 1919 these had grown to include 279 new institutions for children. Similarly, the city of Petrograd had no preschool in 1918, but by 1919, the city boasted 106 new institutions and 180 in the provinces surrounding Petrograd. In other regions the progress was slower but no less significant.[9] Within these new preschools, the teachers experimented with Krupskaya's radical pedagogies, particularly the idea that children should be raised into a culture of freedom. Kirschenbaum explains that "teachers insisted that freedom in the classroom was part and parcel of the Revolution's transformation of social life." One teacher explained that this "free upbringing," as it was called, allowed for the "free development of [children's] inherent capabilities and developing independence, creative initiative, and social feeling."[10]

I could go on citing statistics, but my point is simple: despite the inefficiencies of the planned economy, the paucity of liberal freedoms, and the continued persistence of patriarchal norms, the efforts of many socialist women's activists paid off in the end. Although mostly forgotten today, not only in the West but even in their own countries, their work lived on in the daily realities of hundreds of millions of lives, especially in the lives of women who had opportunities for education, professional training, and work experiences that their mothers and grandmothers had never dreamed could be possible. Even today, the success of socialist women's activism presents itself in unexpected ways, including in the high percentage of women in science and technology in Eastern Europe and in the smaller gender gap in mathematics for girls who live in former socialist countries compared to girls growing up in capitalist ones.[11] In the end, the life and work of the Red Valkyries, the women I've profiled here as well as the many other stories still waiting to be told, made a difference.

What can we, as people who seek justice and equality against the conditions of our own time, take away from this handful of life stories of socialist women in Eastern Europe? In these final pages, I want to pull out a few strands that can help us think through the various factors necessary for living an engaged political life in an era of intransigent global capitalism. In the many years that I have spent reading about and researching these women's lives, I have always been impressed by the importance of role models to them, fictional and otherwise. Inessa, Alexander, and Vladimir Armand managed their romantic entanglements by considering the fictional relationship of Vera Pavlovna, Kirsanov, and Lopukhov in Chernyshevsky's novel *What Is to Be Done?* Lenin and Krupskaya also idealized the stoic Rakhmetov, who rejected alcohol, sex, love, and most forms of comfort so he could hone his body and mind to work for the liberation of the Russian people. Indeed, in forging the personalities of many communists who later went on to become prominent Bolsheviks in the Soviet Union, this obscure novel (that hardly anyone has heard of outside of Russia) essentially changed the shape of the entire twentieth century.[12]

Similarly, Tolstoy, with his writings about nonviolence and personal renunciation of the material world, served as an important role model not only for Krupskaya, but later for activists such as Mahatma Gandhi and Martin Luther King, Jr. One of the first English translations of Tolstoy's *The Kingdom of God Is Within You* found its way to a young Gandhi in 1894, and the two men corresponded by post between 1909 and 1910, with Tolstoy serving as a mentor to the young lawyer.[13] The works of both Chernyshevsky and

Tolstoy inspired their readers to believe that radical political change required a dedicated cadre of acolytes who felt a special calling similar to that which attracts people to religious orders. But rather than working for salvation in the next life, these visionaries demanded social change in this one.

As the characters in Chernyshevsky's 1863 novel and Tolstoy's various writings provided a blueprint for real world activists of the twentieth century, perhaps the lives of the Red Valkyries included in this book can highlight some core characteristics that would-be revolutionaries require for the many struggles that lie ahead. Of course, none of them was perfect; each had their flaws and weaknesses, their shortcomings and failures. But they were real. The fictional Rakhmetov could embody the life of the ideal revolutionary because he never had to worry about paying the electricity bill or managing an underground newspaper. Rakhmetov never achieved power or had to deal with political enemies or grapple with unpleasant dilemmas that undermined his own principles. Rakhmetov never faced Stalin or fought fascists or built an international women's movement. Our Red Valkyries did all of this and more. Here, then, in no particular order, I reflect on the assets and traits that helped these socialist women's activists succeed in the long run.

1. Comrades

All of the women discussed in this book surrounded themselves with a tight network of family, friends, colleagues, and partners who locked arms with them during their many struggles. Alexandra Kollontai's personal networks spanned both generations and countries. Even after her romantic relationships ended, she maintained warm feelings and a willingness to cooperate with the men in her life. She had her son, Misha, and also nurtured a lifelong friendship and made a kind of chosen family with Zoya Shadurskaya. She forged close bonds with fellow socialists Clara Zetkin, Karl and Sophie Liebknecht, Karl Kautsky, and Rosa Luxemburg, and later with Lenin and Krupskaya. In Sweden, she became close with Isabel de Palencia, the Spanish diplomat, and had many friends and acquaintances in the Swedish women's movement. Krupskaya and Lenin had each other, but they also had Inessa Armand, Krupskaya's mother, and Lenin's mother and sisters to support them during their years of exile. Armand had Lenin and Krupskaya, as well as Alexander and Vladimir Armand and her five children. Pavlichenko had her parents, her son, her fellow soldiers, her husband, and, later, a most unlikely friendship with the first lady of the United States, Eleanor Roosevelt. Elena Lagadinova, too, had her husband and three children, her brothers, and the women in the Committee for the Bulgarian Women's Movement with whom she worked for twenty-two years. Beyond her close circle within Bulgaria, she, like Kollontai, maintained a wide network of colleagues among activists and politicians from countries across the globe.

"As we fight together for a world free of exploitation, oppression, and bigotry, we have to be able to trust and count on each other," writes Jodi Dean. "Comrade names this relation."[14] While I agree with her that having political comrades is essential, we should not exclude our wider familial and extended kinship networks from this category. For immigrants, the poor, and communities of color, family networks provide the social safety nets and care that all of us need when we are fighting against insurmountable odds. As important as it is to have colleagues who will join the picket line or show up to the protest, we cannot ignore the important political work of caring for someone struggling with cancer or sharing an afternoon with a senior comrade living alone. Recall when Lenin came back from a particularly stressful congress, seemed to have an attack of nerves, and ended up with a bad case of ringworm. Even as Krupskaya managed party logistics and organized a vast postal network of European leftists, she took the time to paint Lenin's rash-covered body with iodine. Or think of Alexander Armand stepping up to care for the children Inessa Armand had left with him (including young Andrei, the child she had with Alexander's younger brother, Vladimir), or paying Armand's bail so she could escape another imprisonment. The left must not cede the word "family" to those whose only imagination of it is patriarchal and heteronormative. Our families include comrades and, from among our comrades, we often find or make our kin.

I cannot count how many times someone in my life—a friend, a relative, a partner, or a colleague—cared for me when I could not manage something on my own: giving me a ride to the hospital for a procedure, taking care of my young daughter when I needed to travel or attend meetings that ran too late, watching my house for me while I did fieldwork in Eastern Europe, and lending me their cars when mine broke down. They have offered advice and solace when I needed it most. While it should never be the work of only one gender to provide this kind of support (as it has been in the past), we all need to recognize our embeddedness in networks of care and support. These networks include those who intersect with our lives both politically and personally.

Nurturing relationships is radical work. Nobody, not even a celebrated revolutionary like Vladimir Lenin, can change the world all by themselves. The atomization of society into individual nodes of self-interest (no matter how enlightened) perpetuates injustice by dividing us into solitary black holes greedily swallowing the affective resources of others. As important as it is to have a term to name the phenomenon, I dislike the phrase "emotional labor" because it suggests that this labor should be compensated, with its value fluctuating based on the impersonal laws of supply and demand. "Emotional labor" creates a distinction between the use value and exchange value of basic human connection, allowing the long tentacles of capitalism to further wiggle their way into our private lives. Sharing a lazy afternoon with an old friend is just as important as raising your fist at a mass protest (unless, of course, you can convince your friend to attend the protest with you and carry that energy into a long evening). If our goals include making the world a better place for others, we must make the time to nourish our lateral relationships, to cultivate connection and camaraderie. Finding comrades, building trust, and creating community provide the foundation of any political struggle.

2. Humility

For those of us born and raised in a hyper individualistic culture where we play the starring role in the film of our real lives, or in the story of our lives that we create for others online (an increasingly widespread phenomenon which some psychologists have called main character syndrome),[15] the cultivation of humility requires active effort. As we work with others toward a common political goal, accepting our role as a small node in a very complex and dynamic network is essential. Leo Tolstoy reminds us:

> There are two inevitable conditions of life, confronting all of us, which destroy its whole meaning; (1) death, which may at any moment pounce upon each of us; and (2) the transitoriness of all our works, which so soon pass away and leave no trace. Whatever we may do—found companies, build palaces and monuments, write songs and poems—it is all not for a long time. Soon it passes away, leaving no trace.[16]

Of course, there exists a beautiful irony in Tolstoy's words given that his own novels and works have persisted long after his death. In his conception of eternal time, however, even his own work will disappear into the void of an unknown future.

Our hyper-presentism goads us into thinking that our tweets and TikTok videos will provide a permanent record of our deeds and misdeeds, and somehow fix our perceived moments of glory in the ether. As the French-Czech novelist Milan Kundera once wrote: "Everyone is pained by the thought of disappearing, unheard and unseen, into an indifferent universe, and because of that everyone wants, while there is still time, to turn himself into a universe of words."[17]

But when you zoom out and consider that the lifespan of any single person barely even makes a dent in the scope of human history, Tolstoy's clarity about the fleeting nature of existence helps to cultivate the humility necessary to work with others for a greater cause. I'll be the first to admit that Krupskaya's and Armand's subservience to the cause (and especially to Lenin's demands) frustrates me as emblematic of a patriarchal relationship dynamic that contemporary women's activists now reject as sexist and unjust. Unfortunately, women have historically done much of the grunt work of the revolution, and this work must be distributed more equitably if we are to progress. But cultivating a sense of humility in the face of the endless demands of political activism allows us to get on with the business of revolution without ruminating too much on the significance of our individual roles.

Each and every one of the revolutionaries profiled in this book eventually subsumed their egos to the greater cause. Krupskaya willingly assumed the role of deputy commissar/minister of education in order to promote her vision of Soviet pedagogy, whether or not she got credit for it. Armand forfeited the writing of her own theoretical articles for the sake of translating the works of Lenin, and Kollontai eventually accommodated herself to Stalin's reign of terror for the chance to defeat fascism in Europe. Pavlichenko gave up her university studies and dream of becoming a history teacher to risk her life on the front lines, just as Lagadinova left her genetics lab to head up the Committee of the Bulgarian Women's

Movement. "Comrades don't love themselves as uniquely special individuals," Jodi Dean writes. "They subordinate their individual preferences and proclivities to their political goals. Comrades' relation to each other is outward-facing, oriented toward the project they want to realize, the future they want to bring into being."[18] We may or may not get credit for the important work we do, and we have to be okay with that.

3. Autodidacticism

The word "autodidacticism" derives from the Ancient Greek words *autos* (self) and *didaktikos* (teaching), and literally means self-education. In common with the fictional Rakhmetov, who read books for days on end without pause, all of the activists profiled in these pages shared a commitment to continuous study throughout their lives. If we accept Krupskaya's observation that our education within capitalist societies equips us only with the skills and attitudes necessary to survive in a free market economy, then we have to take the initiative to fill up our minds with ideas that challenge the reigning status quo. Kollontai came to her socialism through books: the classic autodidact who plunged herself into a universe of words that offered solutions to the horrors she first witnessed at the factory in Narva. She left her first husband to pursue a higher education in Switzerland, and throughout her life she often turned to reading and writing to find solace in a chaotic world. The young Krupskaya was also a voracious reader, drinking deeply from the cups of Tolstoy, Chernyshevsky, and other writers grappling with the social problems of fin de siècle Russia. She pursued the highest formal education available to her, and then joined various circles where she dove deeper into the works of Marx, Engels, and others. Throughout her life in exile, she immersed herself in the study of pedagogy, and from her memoirs we learn that one of her first tasks was to organize access to the local lending library in all of the cities in which she and Lenin lived. She would later become the mother of Soviet librarianship, and even though she participated in the censorship of books deemed dangerous to the spirit of the new workers' state, she herself amassed a private library of over 20,000 volumes to read and consult for her own work. As she related in her memoir, Krupskaya often held a dictionary on her lap, teaching herself some new foreign language.

Inessa Armand also came into her politics through the secret reading groups sponsored by her young brother-in-law, Vladimir Armand, in Moscow. After Vladimir's death, she tore through a course on economics at a university in Belgium, and throughout the rest of her life she aspired to make her own theoretical contributions to the workers' cause. As a polyglot, she read and translated many of Lenin's works. By the end of her time in exile, her confidence in her own ideas and familiarity with Lenin's corpus allowed her to provide him with constructive criticism, even pointing out instances where he contradicted himself. Lyudmila Pavlichenko was writing her thesis at the university when the drums of war summoned her to military service, and upon her discharge she immediately returned to the university to finish her studies; she later worked up the courage to ask Stalin for an English-Russian dictionary and some English grammar books before she left for the United States in 1942. And Lagadinova, with the highest level of formal education of all of them, continued to read and develop her intellectual capacities throughout her life. From natural science she slid into the social sciences of survey research to better understand the needs of Bulgarian women, and her success at the United Nations attested to her familiarity with the sometimes arcane procedural rules of working at the supranational level. Even in her retirement, she always shared with me some passage or quote from an article or book she had been reading during each of the scores of meetings we had between 2010 and 2017. Autodidacticism recognizes that the acquisition of relevant knowledge provides fuel and inspires creative thinking among those of us interested in seeing the world not as it is but as it should be.

4. Receptivity

A continued life of self-education creates a particular kind of mental flexibility that allows for the introduction of new ideas and points of view. Receptivity requires a willingness to change your mind when presented with new evidence and the ability to think critically about the production of knowledge. Personal and collective growth sometimes requires errors in judgement or tactical failures. Jodi Dean writes: "We can make mistakes, learn, and change. By recognizing our own inadequacies, we come to understand the need to be generous and understanding toward the shortcomings of others."[19] Kollontai is perhaps the best example of receptivity, transferring her allegiance from the Social Democrats (Mensheviks) to Lenin and the Bolsheviks in the face of the brutal violence of World War I. After the October revolution, Kollontai challenged Lenin and Trotsky to defend the vision of the Workers' Opposition, even when it resulted in her diplomatic banishment.

Krupskaya, too, grew out of her youthful Tolstoyan tendencies as she read more Marx and spent more time agitating among the working classes of Saint Petersburg. Armand began her activist career as a feminist hoping that philanthropy could alleviate the suffering of working women, but soon realized that only a complete overthrow of the old order would truly liberate Russia's downtrodden and oppressed classes. The power of ideas far outstrips the power of physical force. Tolstoy explains: "The toiling masses, the immense majority of mankind who are suffering under the incessant, meaningless, and hopeless toil and privation in which their whole life is swallowed up, still find their keenest suffering in the glaring contrast between what is and what ought to be, according to all the beliefs held by themselves, and those who have brought them to that condition and keep them in it."[20] Our own beliefs, no matter how dearly held, can easily become prisons preventing our further intellectual expansion. Receptivity requires the courage to question one's own convictions, even if it means making intellectual missteps along the way.

5. Aptitude

Continued self-education and experimentation allows us to discover our own special competencies and how these skills and natural proclivities can be placed in the service of the greater good. In standard economic terms, human capital refers to the specific investments made to increase the exchange value of our labor power on a free market and so we are used to thinking of aptitude as a commodity. But, as with our emotions, affections, and attentions, we must think of aptitude not only as something we earned or worked hard for, but as a random gift of our circumstances. The famous Marxist idea of "from each according to his ability to each according to his need" views our abilities as social goods because they emerged from a particular set of societal contexts over which we had little control. Access to quality public preschools or primary, secondary, and tertiary education varies widely across communities and countries, as does access to the high-speed internet connections, the paywalled media, or subscription-only academic databases that make modern-day autodidacticism possible. The uneven distribution of mentorship and guidance benefits the already well-connected. Despite these inequities, people come into this world and grow into different skill sets. Part of being a good comrade requires an understanding of where your efforts will make the most impact.

Kollontai was an amazing writer and public speaker, able to craft a moving eulogy or rousing diatribe without any previous preparation. Later in life, she came into her skills as a diplomat and negotiator, a woman able to use her aristocratic background and tastes to further the workers' cause. Krupskaya was a born organizer, a wizard of logistics, and a compassionate listener. Armand enjoyed the gift of languages, moving effortlessly between Russian, French, German, and English to popularize Lenin's writings. Despite her academic aspirations, Pavlichenko had uncommon aptitude as a sharpshooter; so good was her patience and aim that she became an invaluable countersniper, hunting expert German snipers on the front lines. And Lagadinova had tenacity, leadership skill, and the ability to get people to collaborate. Identifying aptitude allows you to hone your skills over time.

6. Coalition

We must be willing to work with people we disagree with, and sometimes this extends to cooperating with people whose views we may find anachronistic. The ability to forge coalitions grows out of humility and receptivity, and it requires patience and empathy for the sake of the larger cause. Over the course of the twentieth century, the moments when the left found its most powerful expression occurred during the life of various "popular fronts" which brought a wide variety of factions together to defeat a common enemy (usually fascism). A willingness to enter coalitions does not mean settling for flaccid interim steps toward the ultimate goal, but it does mean understanding that those advocating for these steps often become further radicalized and can be valuable future comrades. Disdain and derision toward those we consider further behind on the path to radicalization results in their alienation and plays into the hands of enemies who would divide us. As Noam Chomsky says, sometimes it is necessary to simply expand the floor of the cage.[21]

In some ways, the entire history of the socialist women's movement provides an example of long-term strategic use of coalitions on a grand scale. Maneuvering between class-insensitive feminists on the one hand and gender-insensitive socialists on the other, Kollontai, Krupskaya, and Armand had to navigate a minefield of potential disapprobation for pursuing their goal of building a movement that could meet the specific needs of working-class women. Within the framework of the precarious geopolitics of the Cold War, Lagadinova proved herself particularly adept at building bridges with women across ideological divides, focusing on their common goals rather than getting bogged down in tedious rhetorical battles over language and policy. Within Bulgaria, Lagadinova struggled against the persistence of patriarchal norms and the profound resistance of men to helping out around the home. But rather than throwing up her hands at men's stubbornness, she doubled down on fighting for the resources necessary to socialize domestic work. To abuse an old cliché: losing one battle might mean winning the war.

Too often we perceive the ability to compromise and build coalitions as weakness. To be sure, not every situation calls for flexibility and graciousness, particularly when dealing with disingenuous fascists or the single-minded acolytes of finance capitalism. But if the history of the Weimar Republic in Germany teaches us anything, it is that divisions on the left often pave the way for fascists to take power. Between the two of them, the Communist Party of Germany (KPD) and the Social Democratic Party of Germany (SPD) had the votes to prevent the Nazis from winning the plurality in the Bundestag in November 1932. But because Stalin derided the Social Democrats as "Social Fascists," the two parties failed to coordinate efforts. And, if you'll forgive yet another cliché: a willingness to build strategic coalitions means never letting the perfect stand as the enemy of the good. Rather than focusing only on the intersections between movements and identities, socialists must look for confluences, opportunities to build strong lateral relationships between causes that can flow together toward greater justice.

7. Tenacity

In her eulogy for Krupskaya, Kollontai recalls: "Simple and unassuming, she had tremendous will-power, indefatigable capacity for work and great faith in the power of the Party ... In difficult situations or at times of political setbacks, Nadezhda Konstantinovna never lost heart. She has remained an image of unflagging courage and purposefulness in the memories of those who had the good fortune of knowing her personally."[22] Tenacity means showing up, controlling your doubts, and rejecting cynicism and despair no matter how difficult the circumstances. It means repelling apathy within a popular culture context that paints earnest idealism as childish and naïve. Tenacity is Krupskaya getting out of prison and immediately raising funds for illegal strikes. Tenacity is Armand plotting her escape from Mezen when Vladimir's tuberculosis got worse. It is everything about Pavlichenko, both on the battlefield as well as in front of the clueless American journalists asking her about whether she could powder her nose at the front. Some call it "staying power," others call it "grit,"[23] but at base it means carrying on even when you do not want to. It means speaking your truth as you struggle forward whether or not you have a supportive environment around you. It sometimes means getting our feelings hurt: people hanging up the phone, slamming the door in our faces, or trolling us online. In the early postrevolutionary years, citizens who hated her policies literally chased Kollontai off of trams, and she faced almost daily slander in the press. Tenacity descends superabundantly on some while others receive but a scarce natural dusting, but it is a trait that can be learned and strengthened over time: skin thickened and willpower summoned for those inevitable "slings and arrows of outrageous fortune."[24]

8. Engagement

Related to tenacity is engagement: find ways to get involved. In her 1901 pamphlet on "The Woman Worker," Krupskaya argues that women's political consciousness can only be honed through regular participation in action. This can mean strikes, demonstrations, and other forms of civil and uncivil disobedience, but it can also mean publishing, making art, producing memes, or writing revolutionary code. Thinking and dreaming count as engagement if directed outward into the world. Each of the fighters profiled here lived active and engaged lives, although they each made contributions commiserate with their aptitudes. Kollontai gave lectures, organized strikes, and ran the Commissariat of Social Welfare and the Zhenotdel, as well as writing articles, stories, and novellas to promote women's emancipation. In her later life, diplomacy and managing the foreign relations of the Soviet Union consumed her energies. In her last years she edited her memoirs, hoping to leave a testament for those who came after her. Krupskaya taught classes, raised strike funds, wrote articles, published illegal newspapers, managed foreign correspondence, and took care of Lenin's domestic needs while in exile. After 1917, she managed to create adult literacy schools, libraries, reading rooms, and youth organizations while also coordinating efforts to support Soviet women. Armand tirelessly attended congresses, organized underground meetings, carried out covert missions to consolidate support around Lenin, and translated his articles. Pavlichenko volunteered to serve on the front lines as a sniper, and Lagadinova joined the partisan forces before she was fifteen and continued working to build socialism until she was forced into retirement at sixty. Like apathy, inaction suits those who benefit from the status quo. Engagement creates opportunities for tenacity, which grows and strengthens with further engagement: the perfect virtuous cycle.

9. Repose

As much as we need engagement and tenacity, we must also take care not to burn out. Sustained activism drains even the most energetic: Kollontai had heart attacks and Krupskaya suffered from a thyroid illness exacerbated by stress. In both cases their work suffered when they lost the ability to carry on. As head of the Zhenotdel, Armand worked herself nearly to death before cholera finally caught her. Making time to rest and recuperate our strengths must be built into our already overflowing schedules. Even Lenin knew when it was time to take a break and go for long walks in the Alps. Krupskaya's memoirs include descriptions of walking with Armand and Lenin in the countryside around Cracow, and of lounging with them in an autumn field in Switzerland. Isabel de Palencia tells us that she and Kollontai often walked in the woods outside of Stockholm, and even Lyudmila Pavlichenko managed to find time for a week's vacation with Eleanor Roosevelt during her 1942 trip to the United States. And, at least before 1917, Armand allowed herself the luxury of seaside holidays in the south of France and on the Adriatic coast with her children. Repose can mean taking a proper vacation, or it can mean reading a book, spending time in nature, or just hanging out with friends over a bottle of wine. Maybe, someday, someone will build an affordable lefty vacation colony or communal campground where tired activists can gather and recharge, not to further accommodate themselves to unjust structures of oppression but to cultivate the necessary strength and tenacity for the struggles ahead.

The truth is that modern-day extractive capitalism lionizes a culture of overwork that ironically infects even those organizing to defeat it. In the political theorist Wendy Brown's conception of neoliberalism, this all-pervasive worldview has spread economistic thinking into every aspect of our lives as we try to measure, quantify, and calculate the exchange value of everything we do, even if this includes protesting the continued hegemony of neoliberalism itself.[25] In addition to precarious labor in the market, many people have side hustles which require building and maintaining a personal brand. People feel compelled to invest in their own human capital. Affective and social resources become commodities to be strategically deployed for some future (and often amorphous) gain. On top of the demands of self-improvement, we pay the psychological costs of processing the looming threats of climate change or the daily affronts of systemic racism, sexism, xenophobia, and other forms of discrimination. Living in an unstable and unjust world drains our energies and runs us down. Sometimes the best thing we can do is to simply close our eyes and rest. As Jonathan Crary argues in 24/7, sleep can be a powerful political act of refusal against the relentless demands of late capitalism (although I am ashamed to admit that I wrote this sentence at four o'clock in the morning!).[26]

To be totally honest, anyone who knows me knows that I am the least likely to take my own advice about the need for rest. I am constantly running from deadline to deadline on top of a full-time job of teaching and administrative responsibilities at my university. Immersed in a pervasive culture of American "workism" (where work has become a kind of religious calling and forms the basis of our identities), I sometimes lose perspective.[27] I give up sleep, exercise, time with friends and family, and sometimes even the most rudimentary elements of self-care (such as cooked food and showers) so I can finish drafting an article, book chapter, or lecture. I measure the value of my days in things accomplished. I have often pushed myself to the point of utter depletion. Even worse, I have failed in my responsibilities as a friend, partner, comrade, and parent because I drove myself to the point where I simply had no energy and time left to share.

During one of these lows, I found myself in Bulgaria. As I toiled on an eight-year project requiring research on three different continents, I was putting in seven- to eight-hour days in the archives or in the National Library in Sofia, followed by oral history interviews in the evening and then late-night writing sessions. I scrimped on sleep and fueled myself with dried chickpeas, sunflower seeds, Karelia Light cigarettes, and the occasional sesame *gevrek* (a sort of thin bagel). I couldn't shake the suspicion that I was wasting my time to tell a story few people would ever care about: the international networks of solidarity between socialist women in Bulgaria and Zambia during the Cold War.

During that trip, on a day when I was feeling particularly frazzled by the demands of my project, I managed to pick up some last-minute tickets for me and Elena Lagadinova to see *Tosca* at the Sofia Opera and Ballet. I needed to decompress, and I thought she would enjoy the opportunity to see the renovated opera house. Lagadinova rarely ventured beyond her neighborhood in those days, so a last-minute hair dying session preceded our spontaneous outing. I remember her smiling as the first notes of Puccini's overture filled the theater. Together, we sat and enjoyed the production, exchanging but a few words. Although we had been separated by oceans and generations, I marveled that somehow fate had led me into her life. At one point after the intermission, she reached out and placed her hand on my arm. We sat like that for the rest of the show, sharing the pleasure of the evening as we replenished our souls with music.

Elena Lagadinova embodied, at one point or another in her life, all of the traits I have outlined here, even considering her mistakes and missteps and all of the sacrifices and compromises necessary to work within an authoritarian system in which one leader maintained his power for over three decades. From Lagadinova, I learned that the real world is messy and unpredictable. The effort required to navigate unwieldy bureaucracies, to recommit scarce resources, to shape public opinion, and to tackle deeply entrenched systemic stereotypes requires an almost unnatural optimism and willingness to persevere. And as people ignore or forget or utterly underappreciate the efforts that others have made on their behalf, such work is often thankless and draining.

But Lagadinova acquired her fighting spirit as a teenager during the horrors of World War II. She harbored a faith in a brighter future not only for women, but for all oppressed peoples. She spent her life dedicated to that struggle. In this, she shared the commitments of many East European socialist women who came before her, including Lyudmila Pavlichenko, Inessa Armand, Nadezhda Krupskaya, and Alexandra Kollontai. That night at the Sofia Opera and Ballet, as the tenor's voice lilted over the words of "*E lucevan le stelle*" and tears spilled from our eyes, I felt Lagadinova grip my arm, and through her all those Red Valkyries who came before, passing an invisible torch from generation to generation to inspire and encourage the next army of social dreamers. Comrades—all the way back.

Acknowledgments

I would like to thank Angelina Eimannsberger, Maria Murad, Hayden Sartoris, Scott Sehon, Kevin Platt, Annie Finch, Julia Mead, and my daughter for their comments and corrections on various early individual chapter drafts or on the manuscript as a whole. They each provided invaluable feedback and criticism, which motivated me to keep writing. Special thanks to Abby Laform who worked as my research assistant in the summer of 2021 and provided help with the translation of Marcel Body's memoir of Alexandra Kollontai from French into English. Much gratitude to Page Herrlinger and Paul Friedland for lending me their cabin in Maine for a week to put the finishing touches on this manuscript, to Michael Connelly for buying me my very own copy of the Ms. Monopoly game, and to Rachel Connelly for her long-standing friendship. Pope Brock and Sarah Braunstein also provided much needed moral support for the writing process. And Professor Page Herrlinger is a goddess for fact checking my Russian history.

Since most of this book was written during the coronavirus lockdowns of 2020 and 2021, I am especially grateful to the folks who run the Marxist Internet Archive (Marxists.org) for making so much literature available in translation online. Being stuck at home without access to libraries or archives proved quite a challenge, but I decided to push through with this project despite the need to rely primarily on electronically available secondary sources and historical newspaper databases. I used Archive.org, the Hathi Trust, and other subscription databases available to me through the University of Pennsylvania. For the chapter on Elena Lagadinova, I relied on my own scans of her articles and interviews, as well as the copious fieldnotes I'd collected over the seven years that I worked with her. I am grateful as always to the archivists at the Central State Archives and the librarians at the National Library in Sofia. I have written about Lagadinova's life in greater detail in two academic books published with Duke University Press: *The Left Side of History* (2015) and *Second World, Second Sex* (2019), as well as in two obituaries published in *Jacobin Magazine* and *Transitions Online*, and I hope readers will be inspired to consult those texts for more details about her many achievements.

Thanks also to all of the folks at Verso Books who helped bring these chapters into the world, including Sebastian Budgen, Anne Rumberger, Mark Martin, Dan O'Connor, Melissa Weiss, and copyeditor Sophie Hagen. I want to thank Melissa Flashman, my literary agent, for her time, effort, and encouragement, and my wonderful colleagues in Russian and East European Studies at the University of Pennsylvania for holding down the fort while I was on sabbatical.

I would not have survived the challenges of 2020 and 2021 without the steadfast love and companionship of the "quarantine crew," which included my partner, my daughter, and my dog, Daisy. She was the only one of us who seemed thrilled by the advent of the Covid-19 lockdowns in March 2020 because suddenly her people were home all of the time, chopping and dropping food onto the kitchen floor and eating huge bowls of popcorn on the couch as they watched Trevor Noah's Daily Social Distancing Show. A little runt of a basset hound that we rescued back in September 2011, we were never really sure of Daisy's age because she came without records. Over the last decade, my daughter grew up as the hound grew old. When I first wrote these acknowledgements, half a world away from her in Belgrade in mid-November 2021, I feared that Daisy would not live long enough for me to see her again in January. Our little food-obsessed thief didn't make it to December.

Many years ago, when I published my very first book in 2005, I got into enormous trouble with my Bulgarian in-laws because I thanked my two previous basset hounds, Porthos and Tosca, in the same paragraph that I acknowledged my then husband. They thought it utterly stupid to thank two animals who would never be able to appreciate the acknowledgement and used this as evidence that there was something not entirely right in my head. One divorce, ten books, and sixteen years later, *I'm dedicating this entire bloody book to my dog.* Without going full-companion-species-manifesto on anyone, I think it's important to pay tribute to Daisy's role in getting me through the worst of the pandemic. As my partner, my daughter, and I despaired about the plague, mourned for our lost opportunities, and feared for the future, Daisy's insistence on routine, her constant whining, and her ceaseless demands for sustenance, walks, and scritches provided a structure and coherence to our long days indoors. Left to my own devices, I could sit for hours immobile in front of my computer. Daisy always managed to get me up, out of my chair, and back into the world.

Verso kindly allowed me to revise these acknowledgements after her passing, and I am doing so from Athens, Greece, where I recently visited in the National Archeological Museum. Amid their vast collection of ancient artifacts is a rare and curious object: a small marble sarcophagus from the middle of the third century CE. Atop the diminutive box sits an exquisitely carved mature dog, resting in its soft, striped bed. Although funerary statues of this sort were common for people, they are almost unheard of for animals. Still, archeologists believe that someone commissioned this funerary statue to commemorate the passing of their pet pooch. Workmen discovered it in 1937 when they were excavating the north side of the National Garden, which is about a kilometer from where I am writing these words right now. Somehow, it brings me comfort to know that someone near here—over one thousand and seven hundred years ago—felt as mindlessly, sobbingly, gut-punchingly bereft at losing a best friend as I do right now. I have no doubt that Roman era Athenians scoffed at the idea of paying good money to some elite sculptor for a canine sarcophagus. They probably used it as evidence that something was not quite right in the owner's head.

But I get it. And anyone who has ever lost a beloved pet will get it. Daisy kept us all sane and grounded when the world felt like it was spinning out of control. She was more than a companion; she was my comrade. For that—and for her big brown eyes forever filled with the optimism that each day contained within it the possibility of a plateful of unguarded lamb kebabs—I will always remain grateful.

Daisy

Suggestions for Further Reading

There are many excellent books that explore the lives and works of socialist women's activists. This is only a small list of relevant works that inspired and informed the chapters in this book. For more detailed references, please consult the endnotes.

Alexievich, Svetlana. *The Unwomanly Face of War: An Oral History of Women in World War II.* New York: Random House, 2017.

Brown, Wendy. *In the Ruins of Neoliberalism: The Rise of Antidemocratic Politics in the West.* New York: Columbia University Press, 2019.

Bucur, Maria. *The Century of Women: How Women Have Transformed the World since 1900.* Baltimore: Rowman & Littlefield, 2018.

Clements, Barbara Evans. *Bolshevik Feminist: The Life of Aleksandra Kollontai.* Bloomington: Indiana University Press, 1979.

Crary, Jonathan, 24/7. New York: Verso Books, 2014.

Dean, Jodi. *Comrade.* New York: Verso Books, 2020.

de Haan, Francisca, Krassimira Daskalova, and Anna Loutfi, eds. *A Biographical Dictionary of Women's Movements and Feminisms: Central, Eastern, and South Eastern Europe, 19th and 20th Centuries.* Budapest and New York: Central European University Press, 2006.

de Miguel, Ana. *Alejandra Kollontai (1872–1952)* Madrid: Ediciones del Orto, 2001.

de Palencia, Isabel. *Alexandra Kollontay: Ambassadress from Russia*. London: Longmans, Green and Co, 1947.

de Palencia, Isabel. *I Must Have Liberty*, New York and Toronto: Longmans, Green and Co, 1940.

Farnsworth, Beatrice. *Aleksandra Kollontai: Socialism, Feminism and the Bolshevik Revolution*. Stanford: Stanford University Press, 1980.

Fisher, Mark. *Capitalist Realism: Is There No Alternative?* London: Zero Books, 2009.

Fitzpatrick, Sheila. *The Commissariat of Enlightenment: Soviet Organization of Education and the Arts under Lunacharsky*. Cambridge, UK: Cambridge University Press, 1970.

Ghodsee, Kristen. *Red Hangover: Legacies of Twentieth-Century Communism*. Durham: Duke University Press, 2017.

Ghodsee, Kristen. *Second World, Second Sex: Socialist Women's Activism and Global Solidarity During the Cold War*. Durham: Duke University Press, 2021.

Ghodsee, Kristen. *The Left Side of History: World War II and the Unfulfilled Promise of Communism in Eastern Europe*. Durham: Duke University Press, 2015.

Ghodsee, Kristen. *Why Women Have Better Sex Under Socialism: And Other Arguments for Economic Independence*. New York: Bold Type Books, 2018.

Goldman, Wendy Z. *Women, the State and Revolution: Soviet Family Policy and Social Life, 1917–1936*. Cambridge, UK, and New York: Cambridge University Press, 1993.

Gornick, Vivian. *The Romance of American Communism*. New York: Basic Books, 1978.

Harsch, Donna. *Revenge of the Domestic: Women, the Family, and Communism in the German Democratic Republic*. Princeton: Princeton University Press, 2008.

Krylova, Anna. *Soviet Women in Combat: A History of Violence on the Eastern Front*. Cambridge, UK, and New York: Cambridge University Press, 2010.

Lapidus, Gail. *Women in Soviet Society: Equality, Development, and Social Change*. Berkeley: University of California Press, 1978.

Massell, Gregory J. *The Surrogate Proletariat: Moslem Women and Revolutionary Strategies in Soviet Central Asia, 1919–1929*. Princeton: Princeton University Press, 2016.

Masucci, Michelle, Maria Lind, and Joanna Warsza, eds. *Red Love: A Reader on Alexandra Kollontai*. London: Sternberg Press, 2020.

McNeal, Robert H. *Bride of the Revolution: Lenin and Krupskaya*, Ann Arbor: University of Michigan Press, 1972.

Naiman, Eric. *Sex in Public: The Incarnation of Early Soviet Ideology*, Princeton: Princeton University Press, 1997.

Pavlichenko, Lyudmila. *Lady Death: The Memoirs of Stalin's Sniper*. Translated by David Foreman. Yorkshire: Greenhouse Books, 2015.

Pearson, Michael. *Lenin's Mistress: The Life of Inessa Armand*. New York: Random House, 2002.

Porter, Cathy. *Alexandra Kollontai: A Biography*. Chicago: Haymarket Books, 2014.

Raymond, Boris. *Krupskaia and Soviet Librarianship, 1917–1939*. Metuchen, NJ: Scarecrow Press, 1979.

Razsa, Maple. *Bastards of Utopia: Living Radical Politics After Socialism*. Bloomington: University of Indiana Press, 2015.

Rowbotham, Sheila. *Women, Resistance and Revolution*. London: Verso Books, 2014.

Ruthchild, Rochelle Goldberg. *Equality & Revolution: Women's Rights in the Russian Empire, 1905–1917*. Pittsburgh: University of Pittsburgh Press, 2010.

Stites, Richard. *The Women's Liberation Movement in Russia: Feminism, Nihilism, and Bolshevism, 1860–1930*. 2nd ed. Princeton: Princeton University Press, 1991.

Todorova, Maria. *The Lost World of Socialists at Europe's Margins: Imagining Utopia*. London: Bloomsbury, 2021.

Vinogradova, Lyuba. *Avenging Angels: Soviet Women Snipers on the Eastern Front (1941–45)*. London: MacLehose Press, 2017.

Wood, Elizabeth. *The Baba and the Comrade: Gender and Politics in Revolutionary Russia*. Bloomington: Indiana University Press, 1997.

Notes

Introduction

1 Francis Fukuyama, *The End of History and the Last Man*, New York: Free Press, 1992.

2 Abraham Maslow, A *Motivation and Personality*. New York: Harper, 1954.

3 G. Hofstede, "The cultural relativity of the quality of life concept." *Academy of Management Review* 9 (3), 1984: 389–98; R. Cianci and P.A. Gambrel, "Maslow's hierarchy of needs: Does it apply in a collectivist culture?" *Journal of Applied Management and Entrepreneurship*, 8(2), 2003: 143–61.

4 Barbara Wolfe Jancar, *Women Under Communism*, Baltimore: The Johns Hopkins University Press, 1978: 206–207.

5 National Manpower Planning Council, *Womanpower: A Statement by the National Manpower Council With Chapters by the Council Staff*, New York: Columbia University Press, 1957.

6 Kristen Ghodsee, *Why Women Have Better Sex Under Socialism: And Other Arguments for Economic Independence*, New York: Bold Type Books, 2018.

7 Karen Offen, "Defining Feminism: A Comparative Historical Approach," *Signs* 14, no. 1 (1988): 119–57.

8 Sandra Stanley Holton, *Feminism and Democracy: Women's Suffrage and Reform Politics in Britain, 1900–1918*, Cambridge: Cambridge University Press, 1986.

9 Leah Asmelash, "In the New Game of Monopoly, Women Make More Than Men," CNN.com, September 10, 2010.

10 Linda Kinstler, "The Wing: How an Exclusive Women's Club Sparked a Thousand Arguments," TheGuardian.com, October 18, 2019.

11 Ellevest.com/pricing-plans.

12 Robin Bleiweis, Diana Boesch, and Alexandra Cawthorne Gaines, "The Basic Facts About Women in Poverty," AmericanProgress. org, August 8, 2020.

13 Clara Zetkin, "Only in Conjunction With the Proletarian Woman Will Socialism Be Victorious," Marxists.org, October 16, 1896

(published in *Clara Zetkin: Selected Writings*, edited by Philip Foner, translated by Kai Schoenhals, International Publishers, 1984).

14 Sheryl Sandberg, *Lean In: Women, Work, and the Will to Lead*, New York: Knopf, 2013.

15 United States Department of Labor, "Paternity Leave: Why Parental Leave for Fathers Is So Important For Working Families," dol.gov.

16 András Tilcsik, "Statistical Discrimination and the Rationalization of Stereotypes," *American Sociological Review* 86, no. 1 (February 2021): 93–122.

17 Catalyst, "The Bottom Line: Connecting Corporate Performance and Gender Diversity (Report)," Catalyst.org, January 15, 2004.

18 Nancy Fraser, "How Feminism Became Capitalism's Handmaiden – and How to Reclaim It," TheGuardian.com, October 13, 2014.

19 Kristen Ghodsee, *Second World, Second Sex: Socialist Women's Activism and Global Solidarity during the Cold War*, Durham: Duke University Press, 2019.

20 Mary Dudziak, *Cold War Civil Rights: Race and the Image of American Democracy*, Princeton: Princeton University Press, 2000.

1. The Sniperess

1 "Only Dead Germans Harmless, Soviet Woman Sniper Declares," *The Atlanta Constitution*, August 29, 1942, 2.

2 "Russian Students Roosevelt Guests," *New York Times*, August 28, 1942, 21.

3 Lyudmila Pavlichenko, *Lady Death: The Memoirs of Stalin's Sniper*, trans. David Foreman, Yorkshire: Greenhouse Books, 2015, 5.

4 Ibid., 5.

5 Anna Krylova, *Soviet Women in Combat: A History of Violence on the Eastern Front*, Cambridge, UK, and New York: Cambridge University Press, 2010.

6 Pavlichenko, *Lady Death*, 10.

7 Ibid., 20.

8 In 1981, one of these pilots directed a Soviet feature film: *Night Witches in the Sky* (В небе «ночные ведьмы»).

9 Pavlichenko, *Lady Death*, 33.

10 Ibid., 51.

11 Ibid., 72.

12 Ibid., 79.

13 Svetlana Alexievich, *The Unwomanly Face of War: An Oral History of Women in World War II*, New York: Random House, 2017, 123.

14 "Lieutenant Liudmila Pavlichenko to the American People," *Soviet Russia Today* 11, no. 6 (October 1942), available at Marxists.org.

15 Sniper quoted in Lyuba Vinogradova, *Avenging Angels: Soviet Women Snipers on the Eastern Front (1941–45)*, London: Mac-Lehose Press, 2017, 158.

16 Vinogradova, *Avenging Angels*, 200.

17 Ibid., 200.

18 Pavlichenko, *Lady Death*, 82.

19 Ibid., 128.

20 "Russian editor's note," in Pavlichenko, *Lady Death*, xv.

21 Pavlichenko, *Lady Death*, 114.

22 Ibid., 114.

23 Ibid., 141.

24 Ibid., 141.

25 Pchelintsev quoted in Vinogradova, *Avenging Angels*, 35.

26 "Sniper Girl Calm Over Killing Nazis," *New York Times*, August 29, 1942, 17.

27 "Only Dead Germans Harmless, Soviet Woman Sniper Declares," *The Atlanta Constitution*, August 29, 1942, 2.

28 Pavlichenko, *Lady Death*, 186.

29 Ruth Cowan, "Girl Sniper Paints Nails, Powders Nose," *Philadelphia Inquirer*, September 3, 1942, 14.

30 "Famous Russian Girl Sniper Spends Day as Boston's Guest," *Christian Science Monitor*, September 21, 1942, 2.

31 Woody Guthrie, "Miss Pavilichenko," WoodyGuthrie.org, 1963.

32 "U.S. Women Frivolous, Girl Sniper Finds," *Washington Post*, September 17, 1942, 5.

33 Ibid., 5.

34 Malvina Livesay, "The Gentler Sex: Step-Ins for Amazons," *Washington Post*, September 19, 1942, B2.

35 Gilbert King, "Eleanor Roosevelt and Soviet Sniper," *Smithsonian Magazine*, February 21, 2013; Pavlichenko, *Lady Death*, 204.

36 Pavlichenko, *Lady Death*, 204.

37 "Russian Heroine Gets a Fur Coat," *New York Times*, September 17, 1942, 10.

38 Pavlichenko, *Lady Death*, 208.

39 Ibid., 230.

40 "Lieutenant Liudmila Pavlichenko to the American People."

41 Esther Newton, *Mother Camp: Female Impersonators in America*, Chicago: University of Chicago Press, 1979; Judith Butler, *Gender*

Trouble: Feminism and the Subversion of Identity, New York: Routledge, 2006.

42 The Russian name of the film is "А зори здесь тихие."

43 Krylova, *Soviet Women in Combat*.

44 Anna Krylova, "Stalinist Identity from the Viewpoint of Gender: Rearing a Generation of Professionally Violent Women-Fighters in 1930s Stalinist Russia," *Gender & History* 16, no. 3 (2004): 628.

45 General Accounting Office, "Combat Exclusion Laws for Women in the Military," November 19, 1987, gao.gov.

46 "Girl Sniper Gets 3 Gifts in Britain," *New York Times*, November 23, 1942, 20.

47 Pchelintsev quoted in Vinogradova, *Avenging Angels*, 35.

48 "Research starters: World War II Deaths by Country," www.nationalww2museum.org, Accessed November 5, 2021

49 See, for instance: Ishaan Tharoor, "Don't Forget How the Soviet Union Saved the World from Hitler," WashingtonPost.com, May 8, 2015.

50 Vinogradova, *Avenging Angels*, 20.

51 Pavlichenko, *Lady Death*, 236.

52 Ibid., 246.

53 "Lyudmila Pavlichenko (1916–1974): The Deadliest Female Sniper in History," RejectedPrincesses.com; *Drunk History*, season 4, episode 4, "The Roosevelts," directed by Derek Waters, aired October 18, 2016, on Comedy Central; *Battle for Sevastopol* (*Незламна*), directed by Sergey Mokritskiy, released April 2, 2015, by 20th Century Fox.

54 Alexievich, *The Unwomanly Face of War*, 228.

2. The Communist Valkyrie

1 "Madame Kollontay: Heroine of the Bolsheviki Upheaval in Petrograd," *Current Opinion*, January 2018, Vol. LXIV, No. 1: 22.

2 Maria Bucur, *The Century of Women: How Women Have Transformed the World Since 1900*, Baltimore: Rowman & Littlefield, 2018, 16–17.

3 Alexandra Kollontai, *The Autobiography of a Sexually Emancipated Communist Woman*, 1926, translated by Salvator Attansio, foreword by Germaine Greer, Herder and Herder, 1971: 9.

4 Ibid.

5 Bessie Beatty, *The Red Heart of Russia*, New York: The Century Co, 1918, 380.

6   Kristen Ghodsee, "Socialists Have Long Fought for Women's Rights," Jacobinmag.com, February 28, 2020.
7   Alexandra Kollontai, "The Social Basis of the Women's Question," 1909, in Estelle B. Friedman, *The Essential Feminist Reader*, Modern Library, 2007: 178.
8   Alexandra Kollontay, "Communism and the Family," New York: Contemporary Publishing Company, 1920: 21.
9   Alexandra Kollontai, "The Social Basis of the Women's Question," 1909, quoted in, Jane McDermid and Anna Hilyar, *Midwives of the Revolution: Female Bolsheviks and Women Workers in 1917*, Taylor & Francis, 1999: 49.
10 Isabel de Palencia, *Alexandra Kollontay: Ambassadress from Russia*, London: Longmans, Green and Co, 1947, 138.
11 Alexandra Kollontai quoted in Wendy Goldman, *Women, the State and Revolution: Soviet Family Policy and Social Life, 1917–1936*, Cambridge, UK, and New York: Cambridge University Press, 1993, 187.
12 Alexandra Kollontai, "Theses on Communist Morality in the Sphere of Marital Relations," Marxists.org, 1921 (published in *Alexandra Kollontai, Selected Writings*, Allison & Busby, 1977).
13 Kollontai, "Theses on Communist Morality."
14 Kollontai, "The Social Basis of the Women's Question," 15.
15 Kollontai, *Autobiography of a Sexually Emancipated Communist Woman.*
16 Kollontai, "International Socialist Conferences of Women Workers: The First International Conference of Socialist Women – Stuttgart,"1907, in *Alexandra Kollontai: Selected Articles and Speeches,* International Publishers, 1984: 46.
17 Ibid. 47.
18 Kristen Ghodsee, *Second World, Second Sex: Socialist Women's Activism and Global Solidarity during the Cold War,* Durham: Duke University Press, 2019.
19 Barbara Allen, "'A Proletarian From a Novel': Politics, Identity, and Emotion in the Relationship Between Alexander Shlyapnikov and Alexandra Kollontai, 1911–1935," *The Soviet and Post-Soviet Review* 35, no. 2 (2008): 163–91.
20 Lauren Kaminsky, "'No Rituals and Formalities!' Free Love, Unregistered Marriage and Alimony in Early Soviet Law and Family Life," *Gender & History*, 29, no. 3 (2017): 716–31.
21 Faith Hillis created an excellent map of some of these smuggling routes at UtopiasDiscontents.com/Traversing-Borders.
22 "MME, Kollontay, Soviet Diplomat," *New York Times*, March 12, 1952, 27.
23 Alexandra Kollontai, "The Statue of Liberty," 1916, in *Alexandra*

Kollontai: Selected Articles and Speeches, International Publishers, 1984: 112–15: 112.

24 Ole Jödal, "Mme. Kollontay's Career Marked by Excitement and Hard Work," *Christian Science Monitor,* March 3, 1944, 10.

25 Louise Bryant, *Six Red Months in Russia: An Observers* [*sic.*] *Account of Russia Before and During the Proletarian Dictatorship,* Marxists.org, 1918 (published by George H. Doran Company).

26 "Code of Laws concerning the Civil Registration of Deaths, Births and Marriages," October 17, 1918, MSU.edu.

27 "MME, Kollontay, Soviet Diplomat."

28 Beatrice Brodsky Farnsworth, "Bolshevism, The Woman Question, and Aleksandra Kollontai," *The American Historical Review* 81, no. 2 (April 1976): 292–316.

29 Elizabeth Wood, *The Baba and the Comrade: Gender and Politics in Revolutionary Russia,* Bloomington: Indiana University Press, 1997.

30 Alexandre Avdeev, Alain Blum, and Irina Troitskaya, "The History of Abortion Statistics in Russia and the USSR from 1990 to 1991," *Population* 7 (1995): 452.

31 Palencia, *Alexandra Kollontay,* 163.

32 Radek quoted in Leon Trotsky, "Speech in Discussion of the Policies of the Russian Communist Party," Marxists.org, July 5, 1921, (published in John Riddell, ed., To the Masses: Proceedings of the Third Congress of the Communist International, 1921, Chicago: Haymarket Books, 2016, 683–9).

33 Emma Goldman, "Archangel and Return" in *My Disillusionment in Russia,* Marxists.org, 1923 (published by Doubleday, Page & Company).

34 Ibid.

35 Eric Naiman, *Sex in Public: The Incarnation of Early Soviet Ideology,* Princeton: Princeton University Press, 1997.

36 Louise Bryant, "Mirrors of Moscow," Marxists.org, 1923 (published by Thomas Seltzer).

37 Wendy Goldman, "Industrial Politics, Peasant Rebellion and the Death of the Proletarian Women's Movement in the USSR," *Slavic Review* 55, no. 1 (Spring 1996): 46–77; Wood, *The Baba and the Comrade.*

38 Sergei Tretyakov, *I Want a Baby,* Glagoslav Publications B.V., 2019.

39 Fyodor Gladkov, *Cement,* Chicago: Northwestern University Press, 1994.

40 Julian Graffy, *Bed and Sofa: The Film Companion* (KINOfiles Film Companion), London: I.B. Tauris, 2001.

41 Goldman, *Women, the State and Revolution*; Kollontai, *Autobiography of a Sexually Emancipated Communist Woman*.

42 Isabel de Palencia, *I Must Have Liberty*, New York and Toronto: Longmans, Green and Co, 1940, 326.

43 Palencia, *Alexandra Kollontay*, 237–8.

44 Ibid., 237–8.

45 Alexandra Kollontai, "The Soviet Woman—a Full and Equal Citizen of Her Country," 1946, in *Alexandra Kollontai: Selected Articles and Speeches*, International Publishers, 1984: 183–85.

46 Marcel Body, "Mémoires: Alexandra Kollontai," *Preuves* 14 (1952): 12–24.

47 The Nobel Prize: Nomination Archive, "Alexandra Mikhaylovna Kollontay," NobelPrize.org.

48 State News Service, "Foreign Minister Sergey Lavrov's Opening Remarks at the Unveiling Ceremony of a Commemorative Plaque to Alexandra Kollontai," Moscow, Russia, March 28, 2017.

49 Kristen Ghodsee, "The Most Famous Feminist You've Never Heard Of," MsMagazine.com, March 29, 2020.

50 Steven Cerf, 'Fwd: Kolontay.' Email (February 7, 2020). See also: Hans Cerf, "By Leaps and Bounds: The Story of My Life as Narrated to Steven." Europeana.eu.

51 Palencia, *Alexandra Kollontay*, 285.

52 Kollontai quoted in Barbara Evans Clements, *Bolshevik Feminist: The Life of Aleksandra Kollontai*, Bloomington: Indiana University Press, 1979, 272.

3. The Radical Pedagogue

1 Alexandra Kollontai, "In Memory of Nadezhda Konstantinovna Krupskaya," *Soviet Literature* 3 (1989): 153–6.

2 "The Death of Krupskaya," *Chicago Daily Tribune*, March 5, 1939, 16; "Krupskaya, Widow of Lenin, Dies, 70" *New York Times*, February 28, 1939, 25.

3 *New York Times*, "Krupskaya, Widow of Lenin, Dies, 70."

4 Leon Trotsky, "Krupskaya's Death," *New International* V, no. 4, 1939: 117.

5 Robert H. McNeal, *Bride of the Revolution: Lenin and Krupskaya*, Ann Arbor: University of Michigan Press, 1972, 188.

6 Marcia Nell Boroughs Scott, *Nadezhda Konstantinovna Krupskaya: A Flower in the Dark*, Arlington: ProQuest Dissertations Publishing, 1996, 18.

7 McNeal, *Bride of the Revolution.*

8 John V. Richardson, "The Origin of Soviet Education for Librarianship: The Role of Nadezhda Konstantinovna Krupskaya, Lyubov' Borisovna Khavkina-Hamburger, and Genrietta K. Abele-Derman," *Journal of Education for Library and Information Science* 41, no. 2 (2000): 108.

9 Mihail S. Skatkin and Georgij S. Tsov'janov, "Nadezhda Konstantinova Krupskaya: 1869–1939," *Prospects* 24, no. 1 (1994): 55.

10 Ibid., 56.

11 Nadezhda Krupskaya, *The Woman Worker*, translated by Mick Costello, Manifesto Press Cooperative, 2017, 6.

12 Ibid., 8.

13 Ibid., 17.

14 Richardson, "The Origin of Soviet Education," 108.

15 Nadezhda Krupskaya, *Reminiscences of Lenin.* Translated by Bernard Isaacs, New York: International Publishers, 1970:18.

16 Ibid., 25.

17 Clara Zetkin, "Lenin on the *Women's Question*: From *My Memorandum Book*," Marxists.org, 1920 (published by International Publishers in *The Emancipation of Women: From the Writings of V.I. Lenin*).

18 Kristen Ghodsee, *Why Women Have Better Sex Under Socialism: And Other Arguments for Economic Independence*, New York: Bold Type Books, 2018.

19 Donna Harsch, *Revenge of the Domestic: Women, the Family, and Communism in the German Democratic Republic*, Princeton: Princeton University Press, 2008.

20 Krupskaya, *Reminiscences*, 63.

21 Ibid., 86.

22 Ibid., 192.

23 Kollontai, "In Memory of Nadezhda Konstantinovna Krupskaya," 153.

24 Krupskaya, *Reminiscences*, 134.

25 Ibid., 186–7.

26 Ibid., 333.

27 Skatkin and Tsov'janov, "Nadezhda Konstantinova Krupskaya," 58.

28 Nadezhda Krupskaya, "*Concerning the Question of Socialist Schools*," 1918 in Nadezhda Krupskaya, *On Labour-Oriented Education and Instruction*, translated by F. S. Ozerskaya; preface by M.N. Skatkin, Moscow: Progress Publishers, 1985, 47–54.

29 Skatkin and Tsov'janov, "Nadezhda Konstantinova Krupskaya," 59.

30 Lisa A. Kirschenbaum, *Small Comrades: Revolutionizing Child-*

hood in Soviet Russia, 1917–1932, New York: Routledge Falmer, 2001.

31 Norma Noonan, "Two Solutions to the Zhenskii Vopros in Russia and the USSR—Kollontai and Krupskaia: A Comparison," *Women & Politics* 11, no. 3 (1991): 77–99.

32 Sheila Fitzpatrick, *The Commissariat of Enlightenment: Soviet Organization of Education and the Arts under Lunacharsky*, Cambridge, UK: Cambridge University Press, 1970.

33 Jane Womble Gurganus, *Nadezhda Krupskaia and Political Socialization 1917–1930*, PhD diss. (Emory University, 1973).

34 Richardson, "The Origin of Soviet Education," 111.

35 Krupskaya, *Reminiscences*, 370.

36 Skatkin and Tsov'janov, "Nadezhda Konstantinova Krupskaya," 57.

37 Boris Raymond, *Krupskaia and Soviet Librarianship, 1917–1939*, Metuchen, NJ: Scarecrow Press, 1979.

38 Richardson, "The Origin of Soviet Education," 108.

39 Krupskaya, *Reminiscences*, 515.

40 Count Leo Tolstoi, *The Kingdom of God Is Within You: Christianity not as a Mystic Religion but as a New Theory of Life.*" Translated by Constance Garnett. New York: The Cassell Publishing Co. 1894: 49.

41 Nadezhda Krupskaya, "Concerning the Question of Socialist Schools," 1918.

42 John T. Zepper, "N. K. Krupskaya on Complex Themes in Soviet Education." *Comparative Education Review* 9, no. 1 (1965): 33–37.

43 Rebecca Tarlau, "Soviets in the Countryside: The MST's Remaking of Socialist Educational Practices in Brazil," in *Logics of Socialist Education: Engaging with Crisis, Insecurity, and Uncertainty*, edited by Tom G. Griffiths and Zsuzsa Millei, New York: Springer, 2012, 58.

44 Christopher Read, "Krupskaya, Proletkul't and the Origins of Soviet Cultural Policy," *International Journal of Cultural Policy* 12, no. 3 (2006): 245–55.

45 McNeal, *Bride of the Revolution.*

46 Krupskaya, *Reminiscences*, 513.

47 Ibid., 267.

48 Ibid., 268–70.

49 Ibid., 291–2.

50 McNeal, *Bride of the Revolution*, 135, emphasis in the original.

51 "Inna Armand, Friend of Lenin, Is Dead," *New York Times*, July 9, 1971: 34.

52 Martha Vicinus, *Intimate Friends: Women Who Loved Women,*

1778–1928, Chicago: University of Chicago Press, 2006; Sharon Marcus, *Between Women: Friendship, Desire, and Marriage in Victorian England*, Princeton: Princeton University Press, 2007.

53 Vivian Gornick, *The Romance of American Communism*, New York: Basic Books, 1978; Maple Razsa, *Bastards of Utopia: Living Radical Politics After Socialism*, Bloomington: University of Indiana Press, 2015.

54 Ibid., 212–13.

55 Max Eastman, "Lenin 'Testament' at Last Revealed," *New York Times*, October 18, 1926, 1.

56 Gregory J. Massell, *The Surrogate Proletariat: Moslem Women and Revolutionary Strategies in Soviet Central Asia, 1919–1929*, Princeton: Princeton University Press, 2016, 364.

57 Ibid., 361–2.

58 Trotsky, "Krupskaya's Death."

59 Nikita Khrushchev, quoted in McNeal, *Bride of the Revolution*, 281.

60 Trotsky, "Krupskaya's Death."

61 "Winners of the Mohammad Reza Pahlavi Prize and the Nadezhda K. Krupskaya Prize," UNESDOC Digital Library: unesdoc.unesco.org.

62 John Crace, "The Soviet Chocolate Named After Lenin's Widow," TheGuardian.com, January 27, 2010.

63 Louis Segal, "Nadezhda Konstantinovna Krupskaya," *The Slavonic and East European Review* 18, no. 52 (July 1939): 202–4.

4. The "Hot Bolshevik"

1 It is worth pointing out here that I may inadvertently do the same, as there is so much conflicting evidence about Armand's life. I have done my best to cross-reference as many sources as possible, but I do recognize the murkiness of Armand's personal history.

2 Alexandra Kollontai, *A Great Love*, translated by Cathy Porter, Time Warner Press US, 1991.

3 Bertram D. Wolfe, "Lenin and Inessa Armand," *Slavic Review* 20, no. 1 (1963): 96–114; the term "romantic school" comes from Richard Stites, "Kollontai, Inessa and Krupskaia: A Review of Recent Literature," *Canadian-American Slavic Studies* 9, no. 1 (1975): 84–92.

4 R.C. Elwood, "Lenin's Correspondence with Inessa Armand," *The Slavonic and East European Review* 65, no. 2 (1987): 218–35.

5 "Moscow Honoring Lenin Confidante; Newspapers Recall

Woman Bolshevik as 'Real Friend', *New York Times*, May 17, 1964: 23.

6 Michael Pearson, *Lenin's Mistress: The Life of Inessa Armand*, New York: Random House, 2002.

7 Mike Dash, "How Friedrich Engels' Radical Lover Helped Him Father Socialism," SmithsonianMag.com, August 1, 2013.

8 Bengt Jangfeldt, *Mayakovsky: A Biography*, (Translated by Harry D, Watson), Chicago: University of Chicago Press, 2014.

9 Aaron O'Neill, "Life Expectancy in Russia, 1845–2020," Statista. com, October 1, 2019.

10 Frederick C. Giffen, "First Russian Labor Code: The Law of June 3, 1886," *Russian History* 2, no. 2 (1975): 83–100.

11 Letter from Armand dated February 16, 1908, quoted in R.C. Elwood, *Inessa Armand: Revolutionary and Feminist*, London: Cambridge University Press, 1992, 61.

12 Letter from Armand dated August 1908, quoted in Elwood, *Inessa Armand*, 48.

13 Letter from Armand from December 1908, quoted in Elwood, *Inessa Armand*, 66.

14 For a description of the neighborhood where Lenin, Armand and Krupskaya lived in Paris see: "Avenue General Leclerc," leftinparis.org.

15 Cited in Y. Bochkaryova and S. Lyubimova, *Women of a New World*, Moscow: Progress Publishers, 1969: 59.

16 Temma Kaplan, "On the Socialist Origins of International Women's Day." *Feminist Studies*, vol. 11, no. 1 (1985): 163–71; Rochelle Goldberg Ruthchild, "From West to East: International Women's Day, the First Decade." *Aspasia* 6, 1 (2012): 1–24.

17 A free, online digital archive of *Die Gleichheit* is kept by the Friedrich Ebert Stiftung and can be found at fes.imageware.de.

18 An original of the image can be found in the collection of the International Institute for Social History in Amsterdam; See "Stammbaum des modernen Sozialismus" at iisg.amsterdam.

19 Nadezhda Krupskaya, *Reminiscences of Lenin*. Translated by Bernard Isaacs, New York: International Publishers, 1970.

20 Elwood, *Inessa Armand*, 146.

21 Angelica Balabanova (Balabanoff) quoted in Wolfe, "Lenin and Inessa Armand," 101, footnote 10.

22 Quoted in Barbara Evans Clements, *Bolshevik Feminist: The Life of Aleksandra Kollontai*, Bloomington: Indiana University Press, 1979, 155.

23 E. Blonina [I. Armand, pseudonym] quoted in Elwood, *Inessa Armand*, 249, footnote 77c.

24 Elizabeth Wood, *The Baba and the Comrade: Gender and Politics*

in Revolutionary Russia, Bloomington: Indiana University Press, 1997.

25 The full text of this pamphlet in Russian can be found on the website of State Public Historical Library of Russia: elib.shpl.ru. A collection of her works was also published in 1975, I. F. Armand, *Articles, Speeches, Letters*. Moscow, Politizdat, 1975.

26 Elizabeth Waters, "In the Shadow of the Comintern: The Communist Women's Movement, 1920–43," in Sonia Kruks, Rayna Rapp, and Marilyn B. Young (eds.), *Promissory Notes: Women in the Transition to Socialism*. New York: Monthly Review Press, 1989.

27 Kristen Ghodsee, "Rethinking State Socialist Mass Women's Organizations: The Committee of the Bulgarian Women's Movement and the United Nations Decade for Women, 1975–1985," *Journal of Women's History* 24, no. 4 (2012): 49–73.

28 Pearson, *Lenin's Mistress*, 225.

29 Angelica Balabanova (Balabanoff) quoted in Wolfe, "Lenin and Inessa Armand," 112.

30 Emma Goldman, "My Further Disillusionment in Russia," Marxists.org, 1924 (published by Doubleday, Page & Company).

5. The International Amazon

1 Maria Todorova, *The Lost World of Socialists at Europe's Margins: Imagining Utopia*, London: Bloomsbury, 2021.

2 The term "second shift" circulated in the Eastern Bloc well before the publication of the American book of the same name.

3 *Tsentralen Darzhaven Arhiv* (TsDA)-F417-O5-ae496-L34. To cite documents from the Committee of the Bulgarian Women's Movement archive (collection 417) in the Central State Archives in Sofia, Bulgaria, I use the standard form of Bulgarian citation in which F = *fond* (the archival collection), O = *opis* (a sub-unit within the main collection), E = *edinitsa* (an individual folder), and L = *list* (the page numbers).

4 TsDa-F417-O5-ae496, 34.

5 Ibid.

6 "Razvitie na Supermarketite i Hipermarketite vav Frantsiya," Nauka—Tehnika—Ikonomika: Barza Informatsia, No. 76.23.11, from the personal archive of Elena Lagadinova.

7 For a discussion of this phenomenon in the Polish context, see Malgorzata Mazurek, "Dishonest Saleswomen: On Gendered Politics of Shame and Blame in Polish State-Socialist Trade," in

Marsha Siefert, ed., *Labor in State-Socialist Europe, 1945–1989: Contributions to a History of Work*, Budapest/New York: CEU Press, 2020, 123–44.

8 Fredda Brilliant, "Madame Elena Lagadinova," in *Women in Power*, New Delhi: Lancer International, 1987, 84.

9 Amelia Nierenberg, "In Poland, Communist-Era Restaurants Are Perfect for the Moment," NYTimes.com, April 21, 2020.

10 Nevyana Abadjieva, "About Today and Tomorrow," *The Bulgarian Women*, 1977, 2–3.

11 Ibid.

12 "Za Izdigane Rolyata na Zhenata v Izgrazhdaneto na Razvitoto Sostialicticheско Obshtestvo" Reshenie na Politbyuro na TsK na BKP ot 6 Mart 1973 G." Sofia: Partizdat, 1977. For an excellent feminist analysis of this decision, see Savina Sharkova, "Sotsialisticheskata Zhena Mezhdu Publichnoto i Chastnoto (1967–1973): Vizii, Protivorechiya i Politicheki Deistviya prez Sotsializma v Bulgariya." Godishnik na Sofiiskiya Universitet, "St. Kliment Ohridski," Filisoski Fakultet, Kniga Sotsiologiya, Tom 103, 61–80.

13 "Enhancing the role of women in the building of a developed socialist society" Decision of the Politburo of the Central Committee of the Bulgarian Communist Party of March 6, 1973, [English translation] Sofia: Sofia Press, 1974: 10.

14 Kristen Ghodsee, *Second World, Second Sex: Socialist Women's Activism and Global Solidarity during the Cold War*, Durham: Duke University Press, 2019.

15 Central State Archives (of Bulgaria)-Fond 417-box O5-folder AE 496, page 30–31.

16 Jean Lipman-Blumen, *The Connective Edge: Leading in an Interdependent World*, New York: Jossey-Bass Publishing, 1996, 299.

17 A video of Elena Lagadinova's recollections can be found on YouTube.com, "Elena Lagadinova: Bulgarian Women's Activist," youtube.com.

18 Amina Bose, "Elena Lagadinova," *Roshni: Journal of the All India Women's Conference* (VII 1986–II 1987): 49.

19 "The Award of the President's Medal, The Claremont Graduate School to Elena Atanassova Lagadinova," February 27, 1991, from the personal archive of Elena Lagadinova.

20 Brilliant, "Madame Elena Lagadinova," 84.

21 Kristen Ghodsee, *The Left Side of History: World War II and the Unfulfilled Promise of Communism in Eastern Europe*, Durham: Duke University Press, 2015.

Conclusion

1 For examples of this change, see Kristen Ghodsee, *Second World, Second Sex: Socialist Women's Activism and Global Solidarity during the Cold War,* Durham: Duke University Press, 2019; Mary Dudziak, *Cold War Civil Rights: Race and the Image of American Democracy*, Princeton: Princeton University Press, 2000.

2 Aaron O'Neill, "Life Expectancy in Russia, 1845–2020," Statista. com, October 1, 2019.

3 Aaron O'Neill, "Life Expectancy in Bulgaria 1800–2020," Statista. com, June 4, 2020.

4 Aaron O'Neill, "Life expectancy in Albania from 1920 to 2020," Statista.com, June 4, 2020.

5 Aaron O'Neill, "Infant mortality in Russia 1870–2020," Statista. com, October 16, 2019.

6 Aaron O'Neill, "Infant mortality in Bulgaria 1895–2020," Statista. com, April 9, 2020.

7 Boris N. Mironov, "The Development of Literacy in Russia and the USSR from the Tenth to the Twentieth Centuries," *History of Education Quarterly* 31, no. 2 (1991): 243.

8 Fatos Tarifa, "Disappearing from Politics (Albania)," in Marilyn Rueschemeyer, ed., *Women in the Politics of Postcommunist Eastern Europe*, Armonk, NY and London: M.E. Sharpe, 1998, 269.

9 Lisa A. Kirschenbaum, *Small Comrades: Revolutionizing Childhood in Soviet Russia, 1917–1932*, New York: Routledge Falmer, 2001, 38.

10 Ibid., 72–3.

11 Quentin Lippmann and Claudia Senik, "Math, Girls, and Socialism," IZA Discussion Paper No. 11532, IZA Institute of Labor Economics, May 2018.

12 Helen Stuhr-Rommereim and Mari Jarris. "Nikolai Chernyshevsky's *What Is to Be Done?* and the Prehistory of International Marxist Feminism." *Feminist German Studies*, 36, no. 1 (2020): 166–92.

13 Janko Lavrin, "Tolstoy and Gandhi," *The Russian Review* 19, no. 2 (1960): 132–9.

14 Jodi Dean, *Comrade*, New York: Verso Books, 2020, 7.

15 Phil Reed, "The Trouble with 'Main Character Syndrome,' *PsychologyToday.com*. June 1, 2021.

16 Count Leo Tolstoi, *The Kingdom of God Is Within You: Christianity not as a Mystic Religion but as a New Theory of Life.* Translated by Constance Garnett. New York: The Cassell Publishing Co. 1894: 361.

17 Milan Kundera, *The Book of Laughter and Forgetting*, translated by Aaron Asher, New York: HarperCollins, 1996.

18 Dean, *Comrade*, 71.

19 Dean, *Comrade*, 87.

20 Tolstoi, *The Kingdom of God*.

21 "Expanding the Floor of the Cage: Noam Chomsky Interviewed by David Barsamian," *Z Magazine*, April 1997, available at Chomsky.info.

22 Alexandra Kollontai, "In Memory of Nadezhda Konstantinovna Krupskaya," *Soviet Literature* 3 (1989): 155.

23 Angela Duckworth, *Grit: The Power and Passion of Perseverance*, Scribner Book Company, 2016.

24 William Shakespeare, "To Be or Not To Be," speech, *Hamlet*, Act III, Scene 1.

25 Wendy Brown, *In the Ruins of Neoliberalism: The Rise of Anti-democratic Politics in the West*, New York: Columbia University Press, 2019.

26 Jonathan Crary, *24/7: Late Capitalism and the Ends of Sleep*, New York: Verso Books, 2014.

27 Derek Thompson, "Workism Is Making Americans Miserable," TheAtlantic.com, February 24, 2019; Sarah Jaffe, *Work Won't Love You Back: How Devotion to Our Jobs Keeps Us Exploited, Exhausted, and Alone*, New York: Bold Type Books, 2021.

Index

bold denotes photo